I THINK I AM GOING TO CALL MY WIFE PARAGUAY

SELECTED EARLY POEMS

ALSO BY DAVID KIRBY

POETRY

LITERARY CRITICISM

TEXTBOOK

FOR CHILDREN

I THINK

I AM GOING

TO CALL

MY WIFE

PARAGUAY

SELECTED EARLY POEMS

David Kirby

ORCHISES *2004* WASHINGTON

Library of Congress Cataloging-in-Publication Data

Kirby, David, 1944-
I think I am going to call my wife Paraguay: selected early poems
/ David Kirby.
   p. cm.
   ISBN 0-914061-98-4
   I. Title

PS3561.I66A6 2004
811'.54—dc21

                                                    2003056413

Manufactured in the United States of America

Orchises Press
P. O. Box 20602
Alexandria
Virginia
23200-1602

G6E4C2A

TABLE OF CONTENTS

FROM *SARAH BERNHARDT'S LEG*

FROM *SAVING THE YOUNG MEN OF VIENNA*

FROM *BIG-LEG MUSIC*

LATER UNCOLLECTED POEMS

I THINK I AM GOING TO CALL MY WIFE PARAGUAY

SELECTED EARLY POEMS

NOTE

THESE POEMS have been chosen from my first three collections of poetry as well as a ceiling-high stack of magazines which published poems of mine that somehow never made it into a book. For the most part, the poems collected in books appear here as they did upon first publication, although on occasion I have made minor changes or at least changes that are slight in the physical sense; for example, a typical change involves the mere substitution of one word for another, though the new word is sometimes the antonym of the original. Too, the order of the poems as they appeared in the three collections is largely respected, though sometimes I moved a poem away from what I thought an uncongenial neighbor and put it next to a more convivial one. There is one drastic relocation that will be noted below.

The editing process was somewhat different with regard to the uncollected poems. I left the early uncollected poems (i. e., the earliest of these *Selected Early Poems*) largely intact or made only slight changes of the kind noted above. But I couldn't keep my hands off the later uncollected poems; the more they started to acquire the attributes of the poems of my maturity—greater length, more regular stanzas, sawtooth margins, wider narrative swings— the more I helped them along.

A note on the *Rolling Stone* poems: for the last ten years or so, I've been trying to slap the ball into the bleachers; as a result, most of my recent poems have been at least three or four pages long. Since a lot of readers seemed to like these longer poems, naturally I figured I'd better stop writing them and produce some short poems instead. And then I remembered: I already had. Until the mid '80s, *Rolling Stone* published extremely short poems in its record review section, and a very welcoming editor named Charles Perry urged me to send poems whenever I could. I liked doing so for a number of reasons: the pay was good, the magazine was on every newsstand in America, and I kept thinking that sooner or later Keith Richards would read one of my poems (it wouldn't have taken him long) and say "this Kirby bloke's a bit of all right—send him a couple of tickets, someone." Then *Rolling Stone* turned against poetry. No explanation was given, but I can guess what happened; about that same time, a wonderful rock and roll 'zine called *One Shot* went out of business because, as editor Steven Rosen told me, he couldn't stand getting one more poem by some semi-literate huffer about how cool Jim Morrison was.

None of the *Rolling Stone* poems was written in the personal computer era, so I had to endure that peculiar seasickness that comes from working with a microfilm reader in order to retrieve them. In doing so, I noticed a couple of interesting similarities between the six-line poems of my apprenticeship and the longer ones of my maturity. For one thing, the forms were often as regular then as they are now; as simple a poem as "Nightmare #11" has two five-line stanzas, each composed of four two-word lines and a concluding line of a single word. (While I try to get my students to *not* say "I'm really anal, Dr. Dave," I will admit to a certain rigor.) For another, regardless of length, it's the specifics that sell a poem: "How to Get Your Head Shot Off in Tallahassee, Florida" brought in a stack of letters precisely because apparently a lot of readers had licked a dip cone at that Dairy Queen on Lake

Bradford Road. So thanks, *Rolling Stone*, for the encouragement then and the right to reprint now.

Gracious thanks as well for permission to reprint to the publishers of these books: *Sarah Bernhardt's Leg* (Cleveland: Cleveland State University Poetry Center, 1983); *Saving the Young Men of Vienna* (Madison: University of Wisconsin Press, 1987); and *Big-Leg Music* (Washington, DC: Orchises Press, 1995). And thanks to the magazines which first published these previously uncollected poems: "The Alphabet's Good Cheer" (*Pacific International*), "Dimitri Tiomkin, Dimitri Tiomkin" (*Rosebud*), "The End of Poetry" (*Mid-American Review*), "Le Big One de John Dillinger" (*Southern Poetry Review*), "Letter to Borges" (*Southern Poetry Review*), "Monte (Peace in Our Time)" (*Hanging Loose*), "On Being a Poet" (*1996 Emily Dickinson Award Anthology*)," The Possum Boyfriend" (*Columbia*), "Straniero" (*Dominion Review*), "Soft Black Hat" and "The Thane of Cawdor" (*Clockwatch Review*), and "What the Viscount Saw" (*The Quarterly*).

Two final remarks. First, "Saving the Young Men of Vienna" is not out of place, even though it's included in the *Sarah Bernhardt's Leg* section. It did indeed appear in that book first but became the title poem of the subsequent collection because I liked the title a lot and the idea behind it even more. Second, the relocation mentioned in the first paragraph involves "The Potato Mash (More Indefinite and More Soluble)," which is included under "Later Uncollected Poems" even though it appeared in *Big-Leg Music*. But I use the editorial form of poetic license here because I see this poem as a seam in my poetry; it's the last of the early work and the first of the later.

EARLY UNCOLLECTED POEMS

LETTER TO BORGES

Dear Sir: You don't know me, but that's not the point.
I have an idea which I think you can use.
It's not my idea anyway. Here it is:
last night, my four-year-old explained to me,
with unflinching conviction, that the First Man and Woman
were named Wayne and Wanda. Think of it, sir!
As the author of "Pierre Menard, Author of *Don Quixote*,"
in which you describe that friend of yours
who composed "not another *Don Quixote*—
which would be easy—but *the Don Quixote*,"
by which act of deliberate anachronism
and erroneous attribution he enriched
the hesitant and rudimentary art of reading,
surely you can imagine a world in which
Napoleon might be Waldo Davenport
and Caesar turn out to be Bertram T. Watkins III.
And what if God Himself were Bubba or Buddy?
When people prayed, instead of saying
"Almighty God, we implore thee,"
they would say "Hey, Bubba!" And other people would say
"His name's not Bubba, stupid, it's Buddy!"
Of course, you would want all the names to change
at once, see: all the famous people would have silly names
and vice versa. Think of the fun of it, sir! And the justice.

LE BIG ONE DE JOHN DILLINGER

All my French friends want to know
is it true, did Dillinger really have
an eight-inch penis and is it in
a jar, in formaldehyde, in the
Smithsonian? They are obsessed
with measurements, the French,
and I can't help teasing them:
Dillinger's thing is somewhat
larger than an inkpen, I tell them,
the one Camus used to write
The Stranger or Sartre his *Being
and Nothingness*, yet much smaller
than the crusty loaf
the French have each morning
with their milk and coffee.
But they say *non, non,*
pas de plaisanterie, Monsieur K.,
and insist on the true facts.
I'm supposed to do what, now—
lecture them on the sex life
of one of America's most celebrated
gangsters and confirm or deny
that he found the one veritable
poontang *d'amour* that corresponded
to his own prodigious organ,
when there is not even a listing
for "Dillinger" in the *New Funk
& Wagnalls Encyclopedia* that has

answered almost every question I have
ever had? Information is like money,
like sex, there's never enough.

PROLEGOMENON TO A POST-REICHIAN THEORY OF THE COSMOS

> "Men Fake Orgasms, Too!"
> — title of an article in *True Romances*

It started with the women,
spread to the men,
and now everyone's doing it.
Stockbrokers twitch and jerk
on the floor of the exchange.
Waitresses in restaurants
convulse and spill maple syrup
on customers who scream
and fling condiments everywhere
as their phony passion peaks and subsides.
Cowboys fake orgasms
till their hats fall off,
and when their horses buck and rear,
it just means
that horses fake orgasms, too,
mares and stallions alike.

History is altered
as scholars analyze the past
in terms of the Counterfeit Climax:
Hitler was merely faking orgasms
as he thundered at the crowds
in Nuremberg,
and when Galileo
turned away from his inquisitors

and said "Yes,
it really does move,"
he meant the earth fakes orgasms
as she spins around the sun.

Theologians and philosophers alike
speculate that the prime creative forces
have lost interest in us
and that the universe itself
is but a faked orgasm,
a moment of bogus ecstasy
about to come to an end.
I hope this is not the case.
I'd rather we were part
of a true cosmic spasm,
a convulsion
in the divine scrotum or womb
about to fly into the darkness
or open outward
like some fiery astral flower.

MONTE (PEACE IN OUR TIME)

Once I got a postcard from Joyce Carol Oates,
whose novel *Unholy Loves* I had reviewed favorably,
and on it (the card) she wrote,
"I think you must be a fellow Canadian, "
and I figured, well! That's me, all right:
the Mounties, Wayne Gretzky, Margaret Atwood. . . .
It wasn't until years later
when I found the card again
while cleaning up some old files
that I saw she had written
not "Canadian" but "Conradian"
(in fact, I had mentioned a Conrad essay
she'd published elsewhere),
and I thought of the poster I'd seen
for a Monet show,
only the artist's name was spelled "Monte."
I could see this Monte in his plaid jacket
and his open collar and his medallion
nestled in his chest hairs just so,
calling for a corned beef sandwich,
"very lean, please," and a Dr. Brown's Cel-Ray Tonic
so he'd have the energy to finish, say,
Caesar's Palace: The Façade at Sunset.
Names mean too much;
for example, if you called a general "Genital,"
as in, "Your car's ready, Genital—urrk!"
he'd kill you in a fit of rage,
and his bodyguards, confused by the gunfire

and the screaming, would fill the air with bullets
and take him right out of the picture.
Bingo, no more war.

THE ALPHABET'S GOOD CHEER

A is a anything, the compleat democrat,
      the Walt Whitman of letters.
B tells us to go on when the night is dark
      and honeys the harshest word.
C, D, E: vitamins, and besides you want this poem
      to be not a program but a possibility,
Computers Devour Everything. F inspires As
      (fear can be good for you)
while G, which used to tell the horses to turn right,
      just wonders what's under
the costume of the shapely ecdysiast, male
      or female.
H is a glad-hander, I is surprisingly modest,
      J puts the ball
in the hoop every time; K is a superb poet,
      one of the best,
while L is a sprinter, rounding the corner
      toward the Ms,
lickety-split! Now we're in the middle,
      on the median, medium-well,
moving maximally, more fuel, please, Mach 1,
      Mach 2,
oh please quit racing so terrifically,
      you voluble wordsmith
whose every line is an itchy question but never
      the answer
that scratches. Back up, *reculer pour*
      mieux sauter.

XXXs will cover your whys from start
        to finish
where Z sleeps, dreaming of the twenty-seventh
        letter, the twenty-eighth. . . .

WHAT THE VISCOUNT SAW

I was born under the old sky.
We were poor that year and ever after
and offered no entertainments.
Poverty made us
see things differently:
my father began
to put his feet on the table,

and my aunt, my mother's sister,
spurned the viscount, my father's only friend,
and fell in love with Monsieur Amiel,
my preceptor, who went mad with joy.
He died. She died.
They were buried together
in a grave sheeted with lilies.

The viscount still came each day
and stood by the hearth,
laughing and waving his hands,
a candlestick in one
and a wineglass in the other,
painting a thousand airy visions
for my father's amusement

but telling me
I would love a woman one day
more than I loved my own strength and beauty,
but she would be out of reach,

and as he spoke,
I could feel the afternoon
closing around his heart.

Now we are three:
me, my father,
who sits before the fire
with his hat on,
and my mother,
who has never ceased to love him
or to joke about his bad manners.

THE THANE OF CAWDOR

He is usually played by a diminutive if chesty actor,
a regular bullpup of a fellow, almost square,
whereas Macbeth is tall, thin, nervous,
a forward waiting for someone to pass him the ball
or a junior exec who's just been promoted.
Macbeth might as well wear a sign that says "Homeboy"
and the thane one saying "Brave But a Loser";
it's as though the director is saying to us,
Face it, the Thane of Cawdor
is too short to get anywhere in this life.

So why does he die so easily, throwing away
"the dearest thing he ow'd / As 'twere a careless trifle"?
This thane doesn't want to live in a world
where all the big Macbeths shoulder their way through,
taking what they want for as long as they can,
then go down swinging while the rest of us say,
"Yeah, not that bad a guy, kind of a killer, I guess,"
and go for a cappucino, whispering Macbeth all the while,
Macbeth, Macbeth, later stirring in our sleep
and thinking only then
not of kings but of our thane-selves,
brave and unlucky, too good for this world.

SOFT BLACK HAT

I feel like doing something
especially high-minded tonight,
only the little things are the ones
that are often the most attractive.
For instance, you can pull the head off
a mechanical chicken
and mount your friend's picture
on the mechanism and wind it up
and watch your friend bounce around
on the kitchen table until he falls off.
And you wouldn't even have to dress up;
as Thoreau says, beware of any enterprise
that calls for new clothes.
Clothes are nice, though, and sometimes
you can use them to make a point,
as when Toscanini met Richard Strauss,
composer of *Der Rosenkavalier*
but also a Nazi sympathizer,
and said I take my hat off to you
as a musician, R. Strauss,
here removing his trademark homburg,
but as a man I put it on again ten times,
which he did, on, off, on, off,
until he had finished.
That settled R. Strauss's
swastika-loving ass, for sure,
but villains are hard to come by,

especially in a big country like this.
Signor Toscanini was lucky,
since Herr Strauss sought him out
in his dressing room at La Scala
and not vice versa;
with you it might be different,
but scoundrels seldom come to me
for my disapproval.
So maybe each of us should work
on his or her specialty—
conducting, whatever—
and become the kind of person
others flock to, hero and villain alike,
though the latter would not always
look villainous.
Indeed, they'd try to be
as presentable as possible.
Therefore it's our duty
to be better-looking than they are.
We'll be like Toscanini:
artists, humanitarians, snappy dressers.

THE *ROLLING STONE* POEMS

THE PLANET OF NOISE

Didn't get the name,
but I'd like you to meet
my kids Hey? And What?
And this here is
my beautiful wife,
Speak-Up-Damn-It.

THE PLANET OF NIGHT

Everything is
perfect there:
they say
"Bet I hit that
one a mile" and
"Oh, my darling,
surely you
are beautiful."

THE PLANET WHERE THEY DO IT LIKE THIS

Only workers
and students
do it
like that,
then they too
grow old.

LAST REEL

Vampires from space
claw their way
toward America's top
astronaut.
Only one thing
can save him now:
vampires from earth.

THE PLANET THAT TURNED INSIDE OUT

We had such a
nice culture there,

but this dark
is lovely, too.

THE PLANET OF THE DOO-WOP PEOPLE

Harmonize,
you cur,
or die
at the feet
of Queen
Ramalama-
dingdong!

THE PLANET OF LAWYERS

On or about
the first day,
certain life forms
were said to
have appeared.

DESIGNER HAIKU

This week's problem: how
The chairs would look if our knees
Bent the other way.

DAWN ON THE PLANET OF THE SINGLE BARS

Rockets taking off
and landing
all night long,

then silence
and a cool blue sun.

THEY SAVED MARS FROM THE NAZIS

Ah, but their children own it now.

DRACULA'S DOG

He's the
reason why

all the
cats wear

crosses on
their collars

here on
Transylvania Avenue.

APOSTROPHES FROM HELL

Trust no
comma, say
the experts:
it could
be one
of them.

The Exorcist's Press Conference

Sure, there was his side
and my side, but
there were both just sides—

neither of us
took it personally,
you understand.

The lost soul?
Listen, all
souls are lost.

Nightmare #11

I heard
the words
no one
should ever
have to
hear:

"Doctors Moe,
Larry, and
Curly, will
you please
examine the
patient?"

HOW TO GET YOUR HEAD SHOT OFF IN TALLAHASSEE, FLORIDA

Let your hair grow. Put on
a Go Greyhound t-shirt.
Sit at the Dairy Queen on
Lake Bradford Road speaking
French with the two girls
you met in Paris.
Be a little slower getting
to your car than I was.

HOW TO IMPRESS A FRENCH WAITER

Ask for ketchup.
When he says
he doesn't have any,
say "No ketchup?"
in a loud voice
and look around
in amazement.
Teach him a
lesson by leaving
no tip—the swine,
hogging all that
ketchup for himself.

HER PINK SNEAKERS

People are always
stopping her to ask,
"Where'd you get
those pink sneakers?"
What they really
want to know is,
"Which is better,
a boyfriend with a job
or those shoes?"

SELF-LOVE

All day
the dogs raced
across the ice—
food, we thought,
shelter.

All day
they raced
across the ice,
bringing us finally
to more dogs.

VARIATION ON ZENO'S PARADOX

This is my most generous poem.
It embraces everything except itself.

FROM *SARAH BERNHARDT'S LEG*

THE DEATH OF FRED SNODGRASS

San Francisco,
April 6,1974.
It says here
in the *Chronicle:*
"Fred Snodgrass,
who muffed
an easy fly ball
that helped
to cost
the New York Giants
the 1912
World Series,
died yesterday
at age 86."
Fuck you,
Fred Snodgrass.
Some things
we never forgive.

THE BEAR

A bear came to our house one day in the spring.
He sniffed the seats of the chairs and put his head
in the refrigerator. We offered him pork chops
and hamburger patties, but he preferred cereal
and toaster waffles drenched with syrup.

We tried to interest him in an animal show on television,
but he wanted to watch a soap opera.
He sat with his paws in his lap and pretended not to cry,
but big tears rolled from his eyes
and dripped from the fur on his chin.

He stayed on into the evening,
and at cocktail time we poured him a saucer of gin,
which he lapped cautiously at first and then with gusto.
He liked our bed because the mattress was soft,
so we slept on the floor.

As the days went by,
he grew more philosophical and introspective
while we became more bearish, rolling about sluggishly
or snapping at the slightest provocation.
After several weeks we moved out altogether.

All summer long we have been catching fish with our bare hands
and raiding bee hives. Now the leaves are beginning to turn,
and we are getting our cave ready for the long sleep.

It will be our first winter, and we are apprehensive:
what if we don't wake in the spring?

Meanwhile, we shuffle down to the edge of the forest sometimes
and watch the bear go to work, dressed in my old clothes.
He has learned to drive,
though the car lurches and stalls a lot.
We have met some of his friends, and we like them very much,

though several of them resent us,
thinking we planned the whole thing ourselves.
Yet we would have gone on forever in the old ways
had the bear not taken our place.
We owe everything to the bear—that much is certain.

Often at night we talk about the bear
and wonder if he thinks about us at all,
if he moves down the days with nothing on his mind
or looks up at the door from time to time, as we did.
Now we know. Something always comes through.

THE MAN WITH THE RAKE

I think I must have been the man
who stood in the yard last night
and leaned on a rake, feet cold,
gloves wet, not seeing the ambulance
as it drove by slowly and lit
for a moment the outlines of houses
he has never seen, the kennels,
the stables, the kitchen where
Cook makes *daube de boeuf,*
the bedroom where the master
and mistress have disrobed after
riding to hounds and she reclines
on one elbow, breasts loose, as he
kisses her thighs. I must be
the man who enters his own house
to a meal of spaghetti and beer,
who thumbs his wife's nipples
drowsily and sleeps, who wakes
to the sounds of faucets dripping,
who dreams of hawk-headed men
who pull him to the earth and tear
at his genitals, who trudges
to the bus stop in the morning,
lunch pail in hand, or puts out
the milk or throws the paper,
the thick pad sailing over the
hoods of sleek invisible roadsters
and through the kitchen where

Cook is cutting biscuits, through
the walls of the room where
the others lie in untroubled repose,
end over end, its pages filled
with the saving sameness
of things, the world's grace.

LAST SONG ON THE JUKEBOX

It was a song about a man, a woman,
another man, and a car. The man
wanted to borrow the other man's car
but he didn't think it right
on account of his going out with
the woman, who was supposed to be
the other man's girlfriend, on the sly.
The woman didn't care. The man
cared, but not so much that he
didn't borrow it anyway. So they
went to a roadhouse. They had
several drinks, and the band played
rhythm and blues. Then they went
to a motel. Someone who knew the
other man told, but he got the
room number wrong. The other man
broke into the wrong room and
shot a preacher in the leg,
giving the man and the woman a
chance to escape. What could have
been tragic is now seen as comical,
at least with the passage of years.
Today the other man has suspicions
that cannot be verified. He has
sold the car, saying that he cannot
stand the sight of it. The man
no longer sees the woman on the
sly. The woman, who has since married

the other man, still doesn't care.
Neither does the preacher. He was
glad he got shot, he'll say from
time to time; he needed the pain.

AT A FISHING CAMP IN TEXAS

Carla, who works for the CIA,
is supposed to kill you.
Instead she flips over the cage
with the snake in it,
and while the deputies
blast away at the hapless rattler,

you grab the KGB man
in the phone booth,
forcing him to bite the black capsule
before he can recite the Frost poem
which will set his operatives in motion.

Now both sides want you dead.
But you have the KGB man's notebook,
and they know that you too
can recite the poem by Frost.
This is your chance: Carla loves you,
and it's minutes to Mexico.

I Haven't Forgotten T. S. Eliot

When you're daydreaming and you think up these
Anglo-Italian aristocrats and give them names like
Bothwell-Contini and pose paradoxes for them,
that's the Eliot in you.

At night, when the neighbor walks by
your window and you turn, stonefaced, to the woman
who lies with you and say "that's Sir Judas Stukeley
with his bag of traitor's gold,"
that's the Eliot in you.

And when you attitudinize, when you turn off
the TV to whisper something historical, remember:
you can't forget your culture, and that,
old possum buddy, is the Eliot in us all.

MOLIÈRE

You saw a stage being blown across a prairie.
It belonged to the Italian troupe.
Everyone ran after it laughing
until it stopped at the edge of a cliff.

You saw gondolas of gold for Louis.
The Venetians had sledded them
across the Alps,
nearly losing them many times.

Now you are dying. Your chin is red,
and so is the front of your shirt.
Your friends carry you upstairs.
Up they go, up, up.

SAVING THE YOUNG MEN OF VIENNA

How bad it was, how embarrassing, to have been a young man
(to take the young men only) in Freud's Vienna, to go
to prostitutes and get syphilis and gonorrhea
or masturbate and become neurasthenic and then impotent,
to marry and either give new wives these terrible diseases
or dangle before them helplessly, driving them mad.

And even if these young men (again, to take the young men only)
were to make their way through the snares and pitfalls
of sexual development without accident,
avoiding the scarring experiences that turn young men
into fetishists and inverts, still they would sink
to the pavement of Vienna, finally, in sheer Oedipal exhaustion.

Therefore how wonderful it was, how unarguably wonderful,
for Dr. Freud, not just an enormous intellect
but a genius, in fact, though a rather nervous man
in his own right, one so shy that he had to sit
behind these troubled fellows so that he would not have
to be stared at all day long, to listen to their recitations

without directing his attention to anything in particular,
maintaining the same "evenly suspended attention"
in the face of all that he heard, allowing the patient
to drift without aim, without desire,
only interceding to help repetition become remembrance
as the patient surrendered his hysterical misery

and rose, pale and shaken but more certain
than ever before in his life, to go again
into the streets of Vienna and stroll about freely,
greeting old friends, pausing to buy a newspaper
or smoke a cigarette, doing precisely as he pleased,
embracing at last the common unhappiness.

SARAH BERNHARDT'S LEG

Dr. Denucé took it off in 1915,
and P. T. Barnum offered Sarah Bernhardt
ten thousand dollars for her severed leg,
but it was burned or buried somewhere near Dax,
in the Landes district of France.
Years ago I looked in the library
for Sarah Bernhardt's leg. It was not there,

but now I see it wherever I go:
by the side of the road at night;
among the canned goods in the supermarket;
in the back of the classroom, the shoe still on,
the stocking carefully tucked in at the top.
I am afraid it will turn up on my doorstep.
I must find Sarah Bernhardt's leg

before the descendants of Barnum do
or the dogs. Leibniz said,
"Why is there anything at all rather than nothing?"
I say, "Why is there Sarah Bernhardt's leg?"
Love is an act of the will,
according to Augustine—
things count because we say so.

THE VISIBLE MAN

The police won't arrest this guy; he's the visible man.
Women don't scream when he takes off his clothes.
He doesn't have to keep to his room or talk to himself
like a lunatic. He is almost never seen writing
and experimenting with liquids. He does not arouse
the suspicions of many. No one takes him for a criminal
trying to avoid the grip of detection. No schoolteacher
postulates that he is an anarchist. He needn't escape.
He doesn't have to blunder into the house of Dr. Kemp,
an old school chum. Kemp doesn't have to
give him food and whiskey and notify the police.
The visible man doesn't have to chase Kemp
and be overcome by a crowd and killed because he
was never half mad and bankrupt. He had no wish to start
a Reign of Terror. His story is a warning to us all.

KINDNESS AT ICHANG

"... Ichang, where they shipped the night soil from Chungking."

No one stays here long.
Even the Jesus men stopped coming.
But one of them said before he left forever
that the world wouldn't end in fire or waves
but in great acts of kindness,
and as he spoke I saw above his head

a cloud of dust in which the men of Chungking
danced to the sound of gong and triangle.
They took our rakes and crusty rags,
they bathed us, gave us almond cakes and wine.
A woman rubbed sweet oil into my skin,
a child called me Father,
music rose around me like warm perfume,

but I only heard the soil falling,
only saw the ships upon the river.
The sun glowed like an orange
and I longed for nights in Ichang,
the smell of sulfur, home.

LOWELL WUNSTEL

At sixteen he was the only sixth-grader
who could drive: every morning the teachers' cars
pulled into the pebbled lot out back,
and then Lowell Wunstel came along
in his gray Studebaker
and parked as far from the others as possible.

School was boring and safe
when Lowell Wunstel wasn't there, which was often.
The P.E. program
was run democratically—
each term we chose our sports by vote,
and in the spring of that year we picked boxing,

but on the first day,
when Eddie Graham put up his dukes
like John L. Sullivan,
Lowell Wunstel simply raked them aside
with his left hand
and broke Eddie's nose with his right.

Eddie rolled on the ground and screamed
while Lowell lit a cigarette.
The rest of us were too stunned to say anything,
but near the trees a ragged boy yelled
and clapped his dirty hands;
someone said it was Lowell Wunstel's son.

The next day we voted
to play volleyball for the rest of the year.
A teacher pointed out
that Lowell was too young
to have a son that age,
but I never believed her,

just as I never believed
that Lowell went directly from that playground
into the Marine Corps;
I believe that he roams from school to school still
with his gray Studebaker and his ragtag son,
making life tough for others.

Often I wonder if I'll see Lowell Wunstel
in the years to come, and sometimes I think
I'd like Lowell to hit me so hard
that I would never do anything crazy or insincere again,
and every once in a while I imagine him
out there in the darkness, winding up.

OUR MOTHERS ARE COMING

Our mothers are coming out of the earth
in their beautiful white dresses

to take a stick to us, wear us out,
shake us to pieces, make us sorry

we were ever born. They are going to
beat us to death because we've been

cursing, writing on the mirror
with lipstick, leaving the table

without asking, acting like smart
alecks, calling other women "mama."

Of course we'll say we couldn't help it,
we only did it once, it was just

a little one, nobody ever told us,
why pick on me. We'll shield ourselves

as best we can, yelling "Ow, Mother,
stop," not meaning a word.

CANOEING WITH MY SONS

The wind turns us away from the shore
and you cease to be the children
I thought you were.
Bending to the task
with a seriousness that shames me,
you dip your paddles in unison
and pull so hard
that to my astonishment
you lift yourselves out of the canoe.
Kicking and scooping the air
like swimmers rising to the surface,
you strain to free yourselves
from the ordinary,
then turn, laughing,
to wave before going on.
For a moment you hang suspended,
figures in a frieze.
My breaths pain me.
You mount higher and higher,
away from me, toward me.
I will not call you back.

A PARIS EVENING

A schoolboy says goodbye to the last of his companions
and turns toward home. As he crosses the Rue Vignon,
he begins to think of his mother:
her smart dresses and jewelry,
her quick happy movements in the kitchen,
the way she smiles and calls him
sweetheart, angel, treasure.

A block away, a bomb set by terrorists
explodes inside Fauchon. No one is injured,
but all the beautiful food flies into the street:
the eggs in aspic, the *canards aux olives*,
the mussels stuffed with butter, garlic, parsley.
A crowd gathers. Pigeons step carefully
through the *macédoine de légumes*, picking out the corn.
A *clochard* takes a roast chicken by the leg
and waves it over his head in a merry drunken dance.
A man with a briefcase looks around
and slips a tin of caviar in his pocket, then walks away.

The schoolboy has heard and seen nothing.
Crossing the Place de la Madeleine,
he kicks the leaves that have gathered in the gutter.
The streetlights begin to come on.
He is tired now, hungry, dreaming of his mother.

AT MA GROOVER'S

The doors are open at Ma Groover's Pig and Plate
in Valdosta, Georgia, and Ma herself is shelling peas
at one of the lunch tables, waiting for the boys
to leave church early so they can show Ma

their new suits and order some of her famous food:
red snapper, channel cat, stuffed pork chops,
baked chicken and dressing with steamed squash,
green beans, corn on the cob, sweet potato soufflé.

Ma don't like people to look trashy,
so if you come in wearing jeans and work boots,
you'd better count on a bad seat and slow service
and a lot of dirty looks from Ma.

Last night I dreamed I saw Ma Groover
with a chicken bone in her hand; she hit me with it
and told me to go to C. H. Mitchell the Bar-B-Que King
if I wanted to wear my overalls.

So today I will buy a suit. It will be dark blue
with heavy white stitching you can see;
there will be a vest. I will shine my shoes
and eat chicken-fried steak and pole beans

and collards and crackling bread and lemon pie
and iced tea at Ma Groover's Pig and Plate
in Valdosta, Georgia. Let others dress
as they please: I am serious about my food.

In the Dark There Are Shapes Everywhere

A man and woman meet and fall in love
and decide to go to bed together.

They undress, and he feels like a blacksmith
and she feels like a milkmaid,

but when they begin to touch each other,
he feels like a bank teller working late

and she feels like a stuffy vice president
whose true beauty is revealed

once she takes off her glasses
and lets her hair down,

and as he enters her,
he feels like a teenager in the back of Dad's car

and she feels like the new gym teacher
who has been warned about dating the students

but just can't help herself.
They begin to move faster,

and he feels like a renegade priest
and she feels like a nun

whose angry father and brothers
are about to burst in

and menace him with their knives
and pack her off to the country.

As they reach their climax,
he feels like a Knight of the Round Table

and she feels like a queen with a roving eye,
and when it's all over,

he feels like an emissary wrongly entrusted
with somebody else's bride-to-be

and she feels like a king's fiancée
who has drunk a fatal love potion.

In the dark there are shapes everywhere,
eating our sleep.

SUB ROSA

Maps would be literal if the normal order
were other than it is: letters would appear across
the faces of cities, and roads would become red lines.
Pages would fly out of books and then out of windows
to form trees in the yards of the literary.

The trees would shrink to seedlings and then seeds,
which would disappear up the anuses of birds
who would drop them where trees have never grown.
Gasoline would run out of cars and down hoses
into the earth, where it would turn into dinosaurs

who would escape through giant rents in the crust
to lurch down streets crowded with witches,
Manichaeans, Confederate soldiers, Hunkpapa Sioux.
Everywhere things would extrude, exfoliate;
poems would be replaced by their meanings.

As for us, nothing would change.
For already when we lie down together or go for drives
or simply sit across the table from one another,
each look, each word, each touch bears out
the secret history of the world.

DRACULA'S BRIDE

It was on the train
from Vienna to Budapest.
I had just left my husband.
You were reading Seneca
and I *The Imitation of Christ*.

There was a pear,
I remember,
and some cheese,
and when I cut my finger,
you started from your seat.

How nervous we were!
A drop of moisture
hung from your lip,
and your eyes shone
in the gaslight
as you took the pins
from my hair.

That night
a wolf ran beside the train
for as long
as I watched.

AT THE MOVIES

Somehow that's you and your lover up there:
you were expecting *Intermezzo*, not the two of you
stealing kisses in the library or meeting
at seedy motels. You say that you're going

for popcorn and try to find the manager,
but he's not there, and for a minute
you wish you were dead. Then the story
comes up to the present and you see yourself

sitting in a theater. The man you live with
is growling like a bear; come on, he says,
you've got a lot of explaining to do, but you say
wait, wait, I just want to see how it ends.

THE CLAIRVOYANT

I think you must have lived once before as a tree.
A man in a stocking cap cut you down
and pushed you in the river.
At the mill they made planks of you,
and at the factory you became a shelf,
 a coffin, a table, a rocking horse, a door.
These things went all over America
and had long, useful lives of their own,
then each came apart and mingled with the earth again.
How they came together in you is not exactly clear,
nor can it be said where they will go next.
You will be yourself for a while, then what?
The forms are uncertain. The unseen is all we know.

ESTIVAL

Your father mowed today and now your legs itch,
so you stop wrestling with your brother,
who calls you a bad girl and cries.
Then your mother gives you some lemonade,
which you gulp when she isn't looking—
it's the secret anarchy of childhood.

As you pass through the kitchen
you sneer at the dishes by the sink,
the saucers, the plates, the colander,
all straining to be dry!
In the tub you demand more bubbles
and churn your feet, but nothing happens.

Somewhere in the house your brother is still crying.
You mother tucks you in,
and you beg her to tell you about the time
you pulled all your clothes off
and peed on them, and when she does,
you laugh and laugh.

Then your father reads to you
from a big book with pictures.
As you fall asleep you hear your own voice,
though it seems to come from far away,
and it says no, no,
I will not be wed to a frog.

MICKEY'S TEACHER

You change your mind about doing away with Mother,
but she grabs the cup of poisoned tea and drinks it anyway.
Now someone is at the door: it's Mrs. Carmichael,
Mickey's teacher, who has come to talk about his progress in school,
the same Mrs. Carmichael whose sister rode out
to the wheat fields years ago on top of a train
and married a farmer but ran away when he was stabbed
by a jealous rival and disappeared into a crowd of soldiers,
never to be seen again. That was just before the war.

So many crazy things happened in those days:
a Wittelsbach princess believed she had swallowed a glass piano,
one of Wilson's top generals lived in fear of giving birth
to an elephant, and when Chekhov died in Germany,
his body was returned to Moscow in a train marked "Oysters."
All this went right by nearly everyone.
Stepping over Mother as she cools,
chances are Mickey's teacher will never notice a thing.
On the other hand, you will remember her forever.

THE STORY OF THE DEAD DETECTIVE

The anarchist Soto and his men have crowded the hostages
into the art-nouveau conservatory of the Estancia La Anita.
Frightened, then bored, the hostages make up a story
about a dead detective who solves all murders but his own.
The anarchist's men are sheepherders; grim and impassive,

they will be shot by the Argentine Army for what they
are about to do. Outside it is sunny, and the wind is high.
From the window the anarchist Soto can see the Moreno Glacier
as it slides through black forests into a grey lake.
Knowing that he will live, the anarchist watches the glacier,

listens to the story of the dead detective,
and dreams of Spain, a country he will never see.
Later he will own a restaurant in Punta Arenas.
Almost no one will go there. At night he and his friends
will smoke, drink harsh red wine, go on with the story.

THE POEM CALLED HOT DOG, YOU BET

The poem
that will save
the world
is the poem called
"Hot dog, you bet!"

It's all
you'll ever need.
Material wealth
is nothing next to
"Hot dog, you bet!"

Doctors should write
"Hot dog, you bet!"
on their prescription pads
and tell patients
to take it twice a day.

When you ask a librarian
for a good book, he should say
"I've got one
for you right here,
it's called *Hot Dog, You Bet!*"

Soon world leaders
will be setting an example
for everyone else:
the next time
the Pope raises his arms

and greets the masses
with "Hot dog, you bet!"
who among us
will not want to emulate
that merry pontiff?

It's said you can
start a balky car
just by whispering
"Hot dog, you bet!"
into the carburetor.

I saw
a fight on TV
last night
and it sounded
as though

the boxers
were saying
"hotdogyoubethotdogyoubet"
as they pummeled
each other's midsections.

How about
"Hot dog, you bet!"
as a marriage vow?
Why, the simple phrase
would speak volumes.

When my time comes,
I am going to
throw myself under
the wheels of a streetcar
named "Hot dog, you bet!"

and when they lower me into
the ground, I guess
you know what they
will be mumbling
into their handkerchiefs.

The priests will
swing their censers
while the gurus and fakirs
send the familiar mantra
into the sky.

"Hot dog, you bet!"
they'll shout,
"hot dog, you bet!"
as a single dervish
detaches himself

from the crowd
and begins to spin,
wider and wider,
his little skirt
filling the world.

FROM *SAVING THE YOUNG MEN OF VIENNA*

MAN DROWNING IN RESTAURANT

A man is drowning in a crowded restaurant.
Something about his meal upset him,
and he wanted to cry, but he was afraid
that the other customers would make fun of him,
so now he is filling up with his own tears.
Waiters hurry past with cups of soup
and slices of *pâté*, plates of chicken and fish,
ice cream and coffee, while the drowning man
struggles to free himself from his light brown jacket
and cream shantung shirt, tries to kick off
his dark trousers, his brown and white shoes.

He is an embarrassment to his friends.
He will have to drop his club memberships,
his fiancée will break with him,
and almost certainly he will lose his job,
but right now he is trying so hard to reach
the pure air near the ceiling
that he cannot begin to say what it is
that upset him so in the first place;
to drown has become his raison d'être.

The other customers continue to eat;
either everything is to their satisfaction
or they know better than to take disappointment to heart.
The drowning man wants them to notice
how well he drowns, but now they are putting on
their coats and unwrapping the little mints

the waiters have given them along with their checks.
In the half-light of the empty restaurant
the drowning man looks like a dancer
doing something difficult but beautiful
and useless, something to live for.

IN PRAISE OF SAUSAGE

The sun will not rise for an hour,
and the only sound in the kitchen
is the hiss of grease on hot metal
as I put another patty of sausage
into the pan. I am half-asleep and dreaming,
and what comes to mind does so in no order:
the slope of my wife's breasts;
a photo of my father,
stooped and white but smiling,
soon to go before me into the Great Mystery;
the cashier at the supermarket
where I bought the sausage, saying,
"Thank you for not wearing any underpants,
and have a nice day."
Outside the moon is so bright
you can see your shadow. From the window
I watch myself fall out of the night sky,
toward the ground-up things of the world.

I Think I Am Going to Call My Wife Paraguay

I think I am going to call my wife Paraguay,
for she is truly bilingual,
even though she speaks no Guaraní
and, except for "cucaracha" and "taco,"
hardly any Spanish at all.
She has two zones, though,
one a forest luxuriant with orchids
and the smell of fruit trees,
where the Indians worship
the pure and formless Tupang,
who shines in the lightning
and roars in the thunder,
the other a dry plain,
a flat place with the soul of a mountain,
motionless and hard as a rock.
During the day the sun blazes
on the red dust of Paraguay
as dark-eyed, straight-backed women
walk home from the river
with bundles of laundry on their heads,
hoping to avoid trouble,
for the Paraguayans are always fighting;
young conscripts lolling in faded cotton uniforms
have no idea whether they will be summoned next
to overthrow the government or defend it.
My wife Paraguay and I ourselves
had to fight the War of the Triple Alliance,
although in our case

it wasn't Brazil, Uruguay, and Argentina
but Harry, Edward, and Maurice,
her former boyfriends.
I won.
War does not silence Paraguay
or dismay her in any way,
for still her people shout on the football fields
and whisper declarations of love
on the darkened patios of the old colonial houses,
just as my wife Paraguay says she loves me
as the parroquet and toucan fly over
and the perfume of the lime and orange tree
blow through the windows of our big house,
which I call South America
because it contains Paraguay
and is shaped like a sweet potato.

THE DISAPPEARANCE

There is a man in a tea room
in Bath who is saying that
all he wants is a little peace,
and another man, presumably
his son-in-law, is assuring him
that that's what he has,
and the older man is saying
that that's what he wants,
but it isn't really what he wants
because he keeps saying it
over and over again until
the tea room in Bath fills
with his quiet, angry voice
as the other customers
eat quickly and call for
their checks, his voice
following them out into the street
where it cracks with rage
and self-pity but is silenced
at last by voices quieter still
that speak of other things,
of the man who stumbled
into the cave where Arthur
lay sleeping, only to flee,
never finding his way back,
when the king woke
and asked simply, "Is it time?"
or the apparition of the angel

over Mons as the soldiers
marched into battle,
dismissed as an effect
of light and cloud by skeptics
but not by the ones who were there,
who said if only
you could have heard it singing.

AMAZED BY CHEKHOV

Whenever I see a production
of *Wild Honey*, say, or *The Seagull*,
I want to run up on stage
and drink vodka with the characters I admire
and knock the villains down
and have the women throw themselves at my feet.
I forget that the people up there
are just actors who would probably freeze
or hurry off as the curtain descended
and that I would be hustled away by understudies,
eager nobodies destined for nothing better
than television commercials, if they're lucky,
but trying now to impress the stars
by the force with which they hurl me into the alley,
where I bruise and cut myself and tear my clothes.
As for my wife, well!
There would be a study in anger for you!
"You've embarrassed me for the last time,"
she'd say, and that would be the end of,
not a perfect marriage, but a good one nonetheless.
On the other hand, maybe the players would say,
"Marvellous! Wonderful! You're here at last,
old man! Have a drink!"

And that would be my life:
I'd spend the rest of my days acting my heart out
and getting these huge rounds of applause.
I would have to say the same thing over and over again,

but at least it would be brilliant.
And even though something terrible would happen to me
sooner or later, that's simply the price
that would have to be paid by a character
as well-loved as mine. Then *quoi faire?*
as one of Chekhov's impoverished Francophiles would say.
How's this: to get up some evening
when the jokes and the non sequiturs
are flying around like crazy
and make my way to the end of the aisle
as if to go for an ice cream or the bathroom
and get a running start
and fly up the steps
with a big stupid grin on my face
and just disappear into the light.

A TOWN CALLED MERE

There is a little bread
on the plate
and, in the cup,
some tea, about a spoonful—
that's what they have
for breakfast in Mere,
and as for the paper,
it's down the street,
in the yard
of someone
who will glance at it
indifferently, if at all,
because deliveries
never quite make it
to the front door here,
and no one cares if they do;
packages are left
in the driveway
to be run over
and rained on,
and the milk sours
under the dead azaleas.
When the people of Mere
come home from work,
having done nothing,
they sometimes despair
of reaching their own doors
and simply lie down

in a car
or under one,
if all the cars are full,
or in a field
whose name
no one remembers.
No one is ever born
in Mere;
last year, a man
took his wife's hand
in his own for a moment
and let it drop.
Yet no one dies, either:
no one worries
himself to death,
and the people are too lazy
to kill.
And no one leaves:
after all, Heaven
to the people of Mere
would be Mere,
and Hell would be down the road a way,
a little town called Splendid.

CRUSTACEA

Darwin's study of barnacles extended over eight years, 1846 to 1854. In his systematic way of working he generally set aside two and a half hours each day for the barnacles. This became so much a part of the family routine that one of his children assumed that this was what grownup men did and asked the children of another household, "When does your father do his barnacles?"

—George Gaylord Simpson, *The Book of Darwin*

The Neighbor's Eldest Child

Our father does his barnacles in
a somewhat irregular manner,
devoting himself to them for hours
on end and then allowing two weeks
or more to pass without giving them
so much as a glance.
But though he does not do them
nearly so well as Mr. Darwin does his,
nonetheless he takes such pleasure
in his studies that we not only indulge
but emulate his example,
though we prefer quoits and pitchpenny
to shellfish. By "our" I mean the father
of the nine of us, including
Charlotte and Edward, deceased.

The Neighbor Observed

No, no, no. Hmmm . . . ahhh . . . I—hmmm . . .
no . . . I wonder . . . yes . . . I . . .ahh, that's . . .
hmmmmmm . . . blast!

Charlotte and Edward, Looking Down
on Their Father's Exertions

We have learned with regret that,
in the process of doing his barnacles,
our father has lost his traditional beliefs,
becoming a non- but not clearly an anti-
Christian, from there passing through

a period of non-Christian theism
and ending in a nearly but not completely
atheistic agnosticism.
We neither complain nor disapprove,
though we regret that he does not share
our view or expect confidently
to enjoy an immortal afterlife with us.

We died young, by which time
we had absorbed, at our mother's knee,
a belief in the hereafter as perdurable
as the chalk flats on which
our father's house is situated.
Perhaps it is well that we did not live

to do our barnacles as he does his,
for the doing of them would have knocked
our belief on the head,
and clearly it is our belief
that has brought us
to this most pleasant place.

The Song of the Barnacles

Pauvres us!
We are the order Cirrepedia
and kin to all barnacles,
yet different

from those of Darwin
because *nous ne savons pas*
when we are going
to be studied.

For Darwin's lot,
it's clockwork:
two and a half hours
each day.

How know we this?
Très simple:
Their brine
is our brine.

The Neighbor's Wife, Not Without Bitterness

For some months there was a serving girl who would sit on my
husband's lap and kiss him, but that was all. She seemed baffled by
the things he hissed at her: his raptures, his declarations of de-
votion, his promises to leave me and take her away to Italy. I knew
and said nothing. Eventually she became frightened and ran away.
He turned to science. Though his research is fitful, I must say he is
trying very hard. Everyone should have a hobby.

The Neighbor's Eldest Child Again

Let's face it, these are nervous times.
Small wonder that Mr. Dickens,
up in London, and after him
Mr. Robert Louis Stevenson,
will grow rich from their pen-portraits
of the divided self.
Here at home the emphasis is on
being sensible and not running out
to play until your dinner goes down.
A boy at school says his aunt
threatened to punish him
by hanging his cat.
The constable came,
but most of the townspeople say
this was an overreaction;
the cat scratched the aunt
and ran beneath the sofa,

where he has been ever since.
Also, I don't notice anyone
going out of his way
to answer *my* questions.

THE LATE NEWS

The anchorwoman is unsmiling, even somber,
for her biggest stories are about death,
and even when she has a feature
on a twelve-year-old college student
or a gorilla who understands sign language,
there is something tentative about her relief:
she knows that the Great Antagonist
will strike again, and soon.

The weatherman smiles a lot,
but he is making the best of a bad thing,
for the weather is necessary, yes,
but boring. As for the actors
in the commercials, they are jovial
yet insincere, for they do not love the lotions,
sprays, and gargles they urge us to buy,
products that are bad for us anyway and overpriced.

Only the sportscaster is happy, for sports news
is good news: money always changes hands,
and if someone has lost that day, someone else has won.
Should anyone die, that's death, not sports,
and death is the anchorwoman's department.
Even if the Soviets should fire all their missiles at us
and vice versa, the sportscaster will still be happy:
you can't cover everything in a half hour,

for crissakes, and sports will be all that is left.
There will be no jobs to go to,
and our cars won't work,
and there will be no electricity,
but you can make a ball out of anything,
and then all you need is a line to get it across
or a hoop to put it through.
The sportscaster knows how the world will end:
not with a whimper, not with a bang,
but with a cheer.

THE DANCE OF HUSBANDS IN BATHROBES

From the windows of the house
at the top of the hill
comes a stately music;
it is the funeral lament of Palestrina,
mourning his first wife
now that he is about
to take a second, a wealthy widow.

Men shuffle from doorways half-asleep;
it's the Dance of Husbands in Bathrobes.
They have something to say
with their slipper-shod feet,
their awkward hands,
unready for the day's work,
their thin, disorderly hair,
but they do not know what it is.

They advance, pick up the morning paper,
turn this way and that.
Wives and children rush to the window
to gasp and applaud
as the husbands leap higher and higher,
dancing and weeping—
the sun is breaking their hearts!
Look, look, they are sinking
into such sorrow
as only happy men can know.

DRACULA IN LAS VEGAS

As Dracula is killing the pimps of Las Vegas,
begging them not to sell their sisters into bondage,
then flying into a rage and tearing their throats out

when they laugh at him and call him a jive chump,
Elvis is crawling out of the penthouse window
at the Hilton International. Tonight he is going

to make his stand before the over-thirty crowd:
pacing back and forth like a cat-footed killer,
he is going to give them all he's got,

then wipe the sweat from his face with scarves
and fling them into the audience, but right now he
is crawling down the side of the Hilton head first,

wrapped in a red monk's robe over black nylon pajamas and
patent leather boots, his eyes screened
by tinted aviator glasses with the initials "EP"

across the bridge. He reaches the sidewalk
and lands lightly just as Dracula steps forward
and raises a hand as if to say, Stop.

Aaahunnnnghhh! cries Elvis, like a mountain lion
with an arrow in his ribs, as behind him appear
the dead of the desert: the naked Paiute Indians

who bet their wives on the toss of a stick;
the horse soldiers in blue, their skin hanging
from their faces; the Mormons who slaughtered

gentle immigrants from Arkansas on the strength
of a revelation. Dracula shakes his head:
I see you are afraid to face me alone, he says.

Ah've got to have mah power! Elvis snarls.
Ah've got to have mah dynamics!
You lounge lizard, says the sanguinary count,

whatever happened to my Transylvania Twist?
Elvis screams and writhes like a man in flames;
the monk's robe changes color, becomes light blue

and vaporous, like the screens of millions
of television sets on Sunday night when America
sat down in a body to watch Ed Sullivan

wring his hands and bring out Elvis in his prime
along with Lesley Gore, the Doodletown Pipers,
Gary Lewis and the Playboys, and Mary Hopkin singing

"Those Were the Days," then bluer still
as it gathers at the legs and waist, settling over
the shoulders like a jacket from which someone

has forgotten to remove the hanger, the lapels
as lumpy as cold gravy, the suit as blue now as the jowls
of former U.S. President Richard M. Nixon,

whose head floats where Elvis's did,
the eyes wide, the lips silently mouthing the words
I am not a crook then freezing in an inaudible scream

as the dead of the desert burst into laughter
and melt dervish-like into the first rays of the sun.
Something stirs at Dracula's feet: a green shoot,

then another, and another. A carpet of grass
rolls across the desert, a tide of vegetation
broken here and there by shade trees and pools

where the chorines and croupiers bathe, the call girls,
the mobsters come down from their meathooks,
all children again, children in the slowly warming air.

AFTER MIDNIGHT

From the heart of this house
come sounds, the soft bump
of a receiver, the almost
noiseless swish of the cord
against the wall: someone is
hanging up the phone in the
kitchen. Yet you are asleep,
your nightgown bunched
around your waist, and we
are alone, or should be, and
I am afraid, though not for us.
I think it must be someone
who is in great danger.
I think it must be someone
made crazy by pain. I think
it must be someone who has
been wandering from yard
to yard and is now in
our kitchen, calling people in
other cities, other countries,
other worlds, saying *a child
is missing* or *everyone is dead
in there* or *I don't love you any more.*

REVENGE

I think of my enemies
and, in a moment of weakness,
summon the forces of Imperial Japan.

Later I will regret this,
but now it's too late to stop them,
for, having breakfasted

on black tea, rice, and pickles,
having listened to a fiery speech
 by Foreign Minister Matsuoka,

the celebrated Talking Machine,
Mr. 50,000 Words, they move forward,
led by the Nine Young Men of Niigata,

who were so willing to die
they sent their own nine fingers
in a jar of alcohol.

There are hundreds of soldiers now,
each wearing the hachimaki headband
and the belt into which his mother

has woven a thousand prayers
for good luck and a good fight.
At first they are joking,

saying "Don't miss the bus!"
and jostling each other,
but before long their eyes are bright

and they are shouting, "Sleep on kindling,
lick gall!" and "We must have courage to do
extraordinary things—

like jumping, with eyes closed,
off the verandah of the Kiyomizu Temple!"
Now they are running

in full banzai formation,
tens of thousands of khaki-clad men
flashing bayonets, swords, battle flags,

screaming "Punishment of Heaven!"
or simply "Wah! Charge!"
as the Kaiten human torpedoes

tunnel through the azaleas and, overhead,
the Iron Typhoon!
The Heavenly Wind!

the White Chrysanthemum bombers
falling, falling, as I urge them on
in my cocked hat, plumes, braids,

decorations, my gold-headed cane
pounding the ground,
my voice rising shrilly

in a jackhammer stutter,
screaming Suck on this,
you sons of b-bitches, you bastards!

FALLEN BODIES

The night of the Franklinton game
the bus breaks down, the seniors cry
because they will never play football again,
and we all go home with our parents and girlfriends.
Billy Berry lies in the back of my father's Buick,
covered with bruises, unable to lift his right arm,
and tells stories he swears are true:

that apple seeds cure cancer,
that a giant dove hovered over the van
the night his church group came back from Mexico,
that Hitler left Germany by submarine
after the war and established a haven
in Queen Maud Land, near the South Pole.

The air comes in through windows
that won't quite close
as we drive up the dark highway to Baton Rouge,
through towns where tired old men
sell peaches on the corners of used car lots
or doze in diners that sag by the roadside,
spacecraft cooling in the Louisiana night.

THEOLOGY FROM THE VIEWPOINT OF A YOUNGER SON

My younger son, still in kindergarten,
wants to know how Jesus died.
I give him the biblical version,
but talk of scourging and crucifixion
only confuses him, and finally he says,
"I heard he was fooling around with a knife."
If that were the case, I point out,
the New Testament would be another story altogether,
and the magnificent cathedrals of Europe
would be so different, the crosses over the altar
replaced with great shiny blades. . . .

Listen, you little heresiarch,
you're not the first comedian in church history.
Take St. Martin: the crippled beggars of Touraine
took flight at the approach of
his miraculous corpse, fearing the saint would heal
and thus impoverish them, which he did anyway,
just to teach them a lesson.
Or St. Brendan the Navigator, who made camp
on the back of a whale, discovering his mistake
only after he had lit a fire for supper.

The devil is grim, he does not laugh, but we do.
It's not easy being a younger son,
having so many masters.
"We too must write bibles," says Emerson.
Besides, the world is so stupid.

No amount of explanation is sufficient, sonny.
You're right: he was fooling around with a knife.

LOVE IN THE FLOWER OF CHONG

I am sitting in the Flower of Chong,
waiting for my order to arrive
and wondering
how the Chinese fall in love
if, as it's said,
they all look alike.
My waiter has shiny black hair
and eyes the shape of almonds,
but so do all the others.
Yet I am sure his sweetheart
is no less passionate than my own.

I am about to conclude
that love has a spiritual dimension
when my waiter appears
holding a platter
of Wind-Dry Sausage With Raw Lettuce,
and yes, I see now
that he is different
from the other waiters
in a hundred ways,
that he is someone I could pick out
not only in a half-empty Soho restaurant
but in the great market square of Beijing itself,

only now he is casting about in despair,
peering into the face
of one customer after another,
each of us the same.

COMPLICITY

On ne parle pas du corde dans la maison du pendu.
—traditional French saying

A dog kills a chicken
on the farm where I am born,
and my mother ties
the dead bird to his collar.
The dog looks sorry for a day or two;
the chicken, rank and muddy,
is taken away and burned.
And I, who feed both dogs and chickens,
wonder if I will ever have
to face the world with my sins around my neck.

These days I have no dog,
and the only chickens I see
are in restaurants.
I eat them with potatoes and green peas,
and when the waiter whispers,
"Each of us has done something terrible,"
I ask him to be please, be quiet
before the other customers hear:
one should not speak of rope
in the house of the hanged.

THE VERY RICH HOURS OF THE HOUSES OF FRANCE

Our plane falls from the sky
into France, where everyone seems
so much happier than we are,
but no, it's not the people
who are happy, it's the buildings,
the high-beamed Norman farmhouses,
the cottages with roofs of trim thatch,
the chateaux set in verdant vineyards.
The people are like you and me:
their clothes don't fit very well,
their children are ungrateful,
and they're always blowing their noses.
But the buildings are warm and well-lit,
and even the ones that aren't,
the ones that have bad lighting
and poor insulation and green things
growing on the tile, even these
seem to be trying like crazy to comfort us,
to say something to us in French,
in House, in words we can understand.

PATIENCE

His first marriage annulled due to chronic impotence
(though he could masturbate, he said, telling his friends
he had become another Rousseau), he puts it aside forever:

the loneliness, the desire to have someone to come home to,
to take tea with, someone to see. Then the meeting with Effie Gray,
the courtship and engagement, the long ride after the ceremony,

he with a bad cold, she with her period, and, worse, the hair:
Ruskin had seen it in pictures of naked bawds,
but a wife should be as white and smooth as a statue.

They put off consummation, agree to it, put it off again,
associating the act with babies, whom Ruskin finds too . . . *small*,
until Effie ends the marriage, later entering

into a conventionally happy union with the painter
John Everett Millais as Ruskin finds his head turned increasingly
by the thirteen-year-old Irish girl Rose La Touche,

whom he is to court by letter.
Getting no satisfactory reply, he seeks messages from her
through random openings of the Bible,

dreams of her, sees her name hidden within other names,
carries with him one of her letters between thin sheets of gold
and offers it to her at a chance meeting in the Royal Academy.

Rose, anorectic now and soon to die, says "no" as he offers
 the gold-wrapped pages, "no, Mr. Ruskin," again and again.
Seven years later he finds that he cannot stop thinking of her,

and one night he flees Oxford for an inn in Abingdon
where he leaves the door open and, on returning,
sees that the wind has blown the melting candle wax

into the shape of the letter "R."
Beginning a new cycle of hope and despair,
he journeys to Venice, where he takes as gondolier

a horrid monster with inflamed eyes as red as coals
and, setting out for the Convent of the Armenians,
becomes lost in the fog, landing at the madhouse on the island

of San Clemente. There he waits for something, anything,
a voice from the outside. Suddenly there are fireflies!
The black water seems measureless as they flicker and reappear.

THE REASON WHY

If we were to let ourselves fall from time to time
and not always pull the world toward us,
it would take only the occasional misstep
to make us part of it all:
the *felix culpa*, the fall of the Friars Minor
from the high and beautiful tree
in which Brother James of Massa saw them,
the rise and fall of the Third Reich,
the jerk and buck of our own orgasm
as we seem to be lifted by the shoulders
and let suddenly down.
Maybe we should love this way always, like an idiot,
a drunk at poolside tumbling backward into the water,
dragging guests and waiters with him.
Maybe love alone can grab and hold
and be just, pull us under, let us go.

YOU CAN'T ALWAYS GET WHAT YOU WANT

A painter named Jules Holtzapfel blew out his brains in his studio in 1866 and in his suicide note declared: "The members of the jury have refused my work, therefore I am without talent . . . and must die!" But it is likely that Holtzapfel really was without talent.

—F. W. J. Hemmings, *Culture and Society in France, 1848-1948*

The Rolling Stones were right:
You can't always get what you want.
This is true everywhere, not just France.
For example, early one Sunday morning last May,
on KPLM-TV in Palm Springs, California,
a man and woman coupled imaginatively
for eight minutes, then disappeared forever
into the electronic blizzard that blows across "America,"
so named because a German cartographer in Paris,
for reasons best known to himself,
decided to translate the first name
of Amerigo Vespucci into Latin.
Their demonstration of love and agility
never made it to the networks;
millions who learned of it later
were disappointed, and no wonder.
Talent, fame, a little sex on the weekend:
the things we really want are denied us,
and the rest we cannot explain.
Like the old mapmaker, we are all Germans,
each of us lives in Paris,
Italian is what we translate,

Latin is what we write
when we think about countries we will never visit,
guess at what we will never know.

THE VILLA

First there are the wild trees,
the ones without name.
Then espaliered seedlings,
an allée lined with elms,
a grotto with sibyls in it,
a stair bordered by dry foundations,
a fish pool, dry,
stucco figures of fauns with a wineskin,
of a horse attacked by a lion
and everywhere no sound,
not even birdsong,
though a language that expressed everything
was once spoken in these gardens
by people who thought it durable as stone.
They spoke it
until they could no longer
describe themselves.
They used it up,
and now the villa is empty
and hard to see in the half-light,
but in the piano nobile
there are glimpses of ancient landscapes,
of ruins above a bay of water,
of a round temple,
of someone watching—
no, there is a false door,
painted as if partially open,
and in it stands a man in red hose

and brown tunic
cradling a hunting cat on a chain,
its head turned toward a statue
in the foyer of a man
holding a woman by the waist,
and though her body is pressed
against him as in love,
she is looking over her shoulder
at something he cannot see.
In a tapestry, women sitting on a brocade
are conversing with a deer,
while behind them
a knight beseeches a demoiselle
who is turning into a tree;
he begs her, he implores,
but already there is
a look on her face
that speaks without speaking,
that says soon you too will be silent.

LEGACY

Our ancestors leave too much:
habits, reason, their own deaths.
We long to be excited all the time.
Last night at the Tonhalle,
the musicians smashed their instruments,
and this morning I woke with a headache;
when I opened the dictionary
there were more words in it
than ever before.

Still, at any moment I could step out
of this house, which I know so well,
and listen as the birds grow silent in the trees.
One day I will be like them.
And one day you will be like me
unless I leave you nothing,
not even my memory,
not even this poem.

LOOKING FOR THE POEM THAT EXPLAINS IT ALL

Someday I hope to find
the poem that tells me
what is wrong with everybody,
why the beautiful young girls
in horror movies turn to hags
whose skin drips from their faces,
for instance, or why people
drive down the street with looks
of unbearable smugness, as if to say,
"My kids are better than your kids,
they will grow up to be doctors and lawyers,
and I will always drive
this big, expensive car,"
and all the while their coat
is hanging out of the door, torn
and greasy, dragging the ground.
Sometimes I myself hang up
the receivers of pay phones
and tickle the coin return,
a furtive, almost sexual gesture,
only nothing ever comes out
except, once, a small octagonal coin
with a hole in the middle
and markings no one could understand.

CONVERSATIONS WITH THE DEAD

They are not lazy, the dead.
They visit us in our sleep
and ask us to confess to crimes
we never committed.
They remind us of our animal instincts,
how we fought to protect ourselves,
how no one can blame us—
don't be afraid to say "I did it,"
they advise.
One minute they are so nice
that we hope we can live with them
when all of this is over,
but when we do not say
exactly what they want to hear,
they scream and threaten
to lock us up like animals.
After a while we are tired
and want to sleep again,
but they keep taking us back
to the moment it all began,
the night the officer saw her lying there
with her shirt around her neck,
or that cold morning
when the mist rose from the lake,
and they pulled the car out of the water.

FIRECRACKER

It's 1956. Bill Reilly and I
have just bought firecrackers,
and his father is chewing us out
over dinner. Only a dope
would burn up his money that way,
says his father as he lights a cigarette.

Then what does that make you,
says Bill, who is about to put
a big pot of spaghetti on the table.
Pow! The father swings, missing Bill
but not the pot. My mouth flies open:

there is spaghetti on the wall,
on the ceiling, in everyone's hair.
The Reilly sisters cry. Mrs. Reilly faints.
The knuckles on the father's hand
swell and turn gray as Bill charges out
into the yard, bellowing with terror,

and I turn to go. In the driveway I start to run
and then cheer as loudly as I can.
I run all the way home, stopping only
to piss in Old Man Kern's mailbox.
I am twelve years old and happy to be alive.

MORE SHRINES

No, I don't think we would
be orthodox believers
had Charles Martel not turned back
the Moslems at Tours in 732,
thus allowing the West to grow up
Christian, Jewish, and,
for the most part, slightly perplexed
about but mainly oblivious to
such matters as good, evil,
and whether or not we will go
to Paradise when we die.
But even though my hometown
of Tallahassee contains the name
of Allah, and even though
we have Arabic words in our language,
such as algebra, which sounds
Arabic and even looks that way,
or did in the eighth grade,
still, this is America,
and while I cannot see us adopting
the placid temperaments of
the desert people, so self-composed
in their long, loose robes
yet struggling continuously with
the malicious djinn who rule
the kingdom of death that begins
just a few feet from the oasis,
we need, do we not,

more places in this country
that are solemn and serene,
although there can be only one holy stone
set in the corner of the Ka'aba
in Mecca, white when given
to Adam at the time of the fall
but black now from the sins of
those who have kissed it.
I like this: a kind of sin-magnet
that would pull all of
the wickedness out of us,
because, as it says in the Koran,
you can run, pretty momma,
but you can't hide.

Money Is Falling Out of Our Mouths

As Dostoevsky said,
one sacred memory
from childhood
is perhaps
the best education of all.

Maybe that's what
my son was talking about
when he glanced around
at dinner the other night
and whispered,
"We look like millionaires."

Once I overheard
my mother murmuring
to my father,
and I asked her
what she had said;

she blushed
and looked at the ground
and asked,
"Can't a husband
and wife have secrets?"

Husband! Wife!
How those words burned me!
In that moment

I lost the power of speech,
and it was years
before I got it back.

RUSSIA

A woman lifts a wine bottle
and brings it down
on the head of her lover,
who falls dead at her feet.

At the trial a student
leaps up, pale with love,
and shouts I did it,
so they take him away.

When he gets out of prison,
he goes down to the river,
where he sees the woman
reading under a tree.

She has become
a young girl again.
He offers her a bouquet
and says marry me, marry me

but she throws the flowers
in the water and says nothing.
It is the most beautiful
day of his life.

TRANSMUTATION AS A FACT OF LIFE

Forget the mysteries of mineral prudence,
the chemical weddings, the sympathetic powders
that cure wounds at a distance,
the stone at the heart of the Alchemical Citadel,
guarded by a dragon, attainable only by the silent,
the faithful, the pure of heart—

it's enough to know that when Albertus Magnus
gave a dinner for the Count of Holland,
the table was set in the snow-covered garden
of the monastery, and as the startled guests
took their places, warm breezes blew,
and spring flowers pushed up through the frozen earth.

Oh, Ko Hung of China, Thrice-Great Hermes,
do rocks not copulate, give birth, and die?
Strike me with iron tempered
in the urine of a small, red-headed boy
if we are not, all of us,
trying to do something about the weather.

MOTHERS AND FATHERS

In old photographs they are dark-browed,
their eyes set deeply in faces shadowed
by the brims of hats no longer fashionable.
The years go by; they become lighter

and, finally, white. Each day
they are more and more transparent,
and soon we will not be able to see them at all.
Oh, we shall hear the rustle of clothing

in other rooms, but when we look,
no one will be there; the phone will ring,
but when we pick it up, no one will answer.
At the last minute they will appear again,

and we shall reach for them,
but the wind will blow them away,
like the hollow scapes of the dandelion,
floating forever on the dry air.

THE COWS ARE GOING TO PARIS: A PASTORAL

The cows are going to Paris;
when they boarded the train
at Corbeil and Fontainebleau,
the people were frightened
and ran out into the fields and meadows
and chewed the grass in terror,

and now the cows are going
to shop at the Galeries Lafayette,
stroll in the Louvre and the Jeu de Paume,
see plays produced and directed by cows,
a farce in the manner
of Georges Feydeau, for example,

in which a certain Monsieur Bull
wishes to deceive his wife,
so he arranges to meet the wife
of a friend in a hotel of low repute.
The only one who can betray him
is another monsieur who stutters

whenever it rains.
And of course it rains:
"M-m-mooo!" he says, "M-m-m-moooo!"
The cows are delighted;
they have never thought of the rain
as having so much meaning until now.

And when the deceived monsieur
grabs a sword in order
to pierce the innards of his false friend,
the cows are absolutely enthralled,
it having never occurred to them
that the slaughter of their species

could be occasioned by anything
other than the desire to eat
or make money, that it could have
rage as its cause,
a feeling of betrayal,
the breaking of a heart.

Meanwhile, the people from the train
have made themselves comfortable
under the trees;
the diet of the cows
is nourishing and unrefined,

and somehow it seems natural
to stand in small groups for hours,
saying nothing. Indeed,
when the cows return
to the fields and meadows,

the people will not get back on board
and must be prodded
before they enter the cars.

Having been to the city, the cows understand;
to them, the people are like

the nymphs and shepherds in the painting
by Watteau who are made to leave
the isle of forgetfulness and so set out
for the fallen world, but slowly,
and not without a mournful backward glance.

FROM *BIG-LEG MUSIC*

LET'S GET LOST

In Honolulu I am watching a movie called *Let's Get Lost*.
First I have a question for Hawai'i, though:
how could you possibly be a state? For you are not Kansas
or even Missouri, even though your money is the same

as theirs and so are the stamps. While we wait
for the answer to that one, let's get back to the movie.
Let's Get Lost is about a handsome jazz trumpeter
named Chet Baker who got hooked on heroin and

had his teeth knocked out and made a big comeback
years later, though by then he was toothless
and his face was as lined as the mountains
overlooking the leeward shore of Oahu.

In Hawai'i you are either a haole, that is, "ghost"
or white person, or a local. Or a hapa-haole,
which means mixed breed. I call myself hapa-haole
because half of me is a ghost, yet the other is, not local blood,

but nothing, because I'm still working on that other half—
I haven't lost it yet because I've never really found it.
This is what you do when you're not a great jazz trumpeter:
try to get what you don't have and not let other people know

what you're doing. Meanwhile, here's Hawai'i's answer
to my question: I'm a state because everybody says so.
That makes sense: you are whatever a lot of people say you are,
which is why people are happiest in crowds,

121

in shopping malls, say, or sports stadiums.
Otherwise, you're outnumbered, with your haole half overshadowed
by the nothing half, which potentially includes Everything.
Chet Baker was mean to everyone: he alienated his lovers,

and his three grown children sound angry and worthless.
They were the ones who seem lost: what Chet Baker had done
was lose those parts of himself that he didn't need—
everybody around him needed them, but he didn't.

Nietzsche: "When virtue has slept, she will get up more refreshed."
In Chet Baker's case, virtue never woke up at all,
whereas in the rest of us it never really sleeps;
it tosses and turns and makes itself miserable and us, too.

Hawai'i, I salute you. You're some place to visit,
and I would get lost in you if I had the money.
As the lights come up, part of me says do the right thing.
But the other part says, if you get lost, stay lost.

BROKEN PROMISES

I have met them in dark alleys, limping and one-armed;
I have seem them playing cards under a single light-bulb
and tried to join in, but they refused me rudely,
knowing I would only let them win.
I have seen them in the foyers of theaters,
coming back late from the interval
long after the others have taken their seats,
and in deserted shopping malls late at night,
peering at things they can never buy,
and I have found them wandering
in a wood where I too have wandered.
This morning I caught one;
small and stupid, too slow to get away,
it was only a promise I had made to myself once
and then forgot, but it screamed and kicked at me
and ran to join the others, who looked at me with reproach
in their long, sad faces.
When I drew near them, they scurried away,
even though they will sleep in my yard tonight.
I hate them for their ingratitude,
I who have kept countless promises,
as dead now as Shakespeare's children.
"You bastards," I scream,
"you have to love me—I gave you life!"

YOUR MOMMA SAYS OMNIA VINCIT AMOR

Running down the Via degli Annibaldi
I hear Aretha say
my momma said leave you alone
and as I hurry up the steps
of the church of San Pietro in Vincoli
I hear her say my daddy said come on home
and as I turn to go down the right aisle
she says my doctor said take it easy
and then I stop right in front
of Michelangelo's *Moses*:
oh but your loving is much too strong
for these chain chain chains
which were used to bind St. Peter in Palestine
and are themselves preserved under glass
in the same church. Moses is angry;
he's just seen the Israelites
dancing around the Golden Calf
and now he twists his beard with his right hand
and shifts his weight to the ball of his left foot
so he can jump up and smash the stone tablets
with the Ten Commandments on them.

I'd like to be that angry just once—
or, like Bernini's St. Teresa,
to pass out from pleasure! I think of Bo Diddley
as I scurry down the Via XX Settembre
and up the steps of the church of Santa Maria della Vittoria
with its great Baroque sculpture

in which the angel smiles at the saint
as sweetly as a child would, yet his copper arrow
is aimed between her legs;
God might as well have told Teresa
he walked forty-seven miles of barbed wire,
got a cobra snake for a necktie
and a house by the roadside made out of rattlesnake hide
because, really, the only question is,
Who do you love?

WHITE

I am the whitest person I know,
even though my name is Kirby,
not White, which is the name
of millions of Anglophones,
not to mention
all the Weisses, LeBlancs,
and LoBiancos, each of them
as different as can be yet
all bearing this deceptive name
with its calm surface and
its secret allegiance to itself.

For instance, everyone loves
white bread, certainly when
they are young, yet by the time
they have come to prefer wheat,
rye, or pumpernickel, an educated
few, at least, have learned
to love the White Whale, who
stands for everything, including
a number of things that are
quite terrible; Melville himself
said so. From an electromagnetic
standpoint, white is not one

but all colors, even though
we cannot see them any more
than we can see the white

and dimpled buttocks of the nuns
who work in the garden,
their hands as dark and wrinkled
as the earth itself, the skin
beneath their habits as pale
and smooth as that of the Baby
they will meet some day,
the day of the death of
their whiteness, the birth
of all whiteness everywhere.

BEGINNING WITH A LINE BY E. M. FORSTER

A friendliness, as of dwarfs shaking hands, was in
     the air:
the two men meeting for the first time, the one
     who had
carved "I love Felicia" on the desk top and
     the one
who had added "Me, too!" in smaller letters
     below. Each
was of normal height in the common sense, though each
     had been
dwarfed by his love for Felicia, of whom
     nothing was
known, not even if she existed except as
     a bond

between the two men, who may have made her up
     in order
to form a club dedicated to the word
     amor, love
perfect and unchanging, as though carved in precious
     stone and
hung on the breast of a beauty in a
     gallery, long
ago—that is to say, they met as giants,
     grotesque and
triumphant, and one didn't know whether to
     pity or
envy them or extend a hand and say, "I too
     loved her."

EINE GÖTTERDÄMMERUNG IN MUDVILLE

This time he'll do it, they think—
tear the cover off the ball
like the much-despised Blake
or at least, like Flynn,
get a single.

And then it's over.
Days pass, months, years.
They turn and look at each other
as though each
remembers something:

Virgil's *Eclogues*,
the paintings
of Poussin
and Watteau, Balzac's
Comédie Humaine. . . .

As though each has seen
the god lie down heavily
beneath the trees, breathless,
the flesh thick
on his still-beautiful body.

Virginia Rilke

Each day I park my car
      and walk through crowds
of girls and boys on their way to school.
      The girls, who laugh and kid each other,
talk about the boys
      but also their diets and other girls.
The boys, who are grim and unsmiling,
      talk about pussy
but also sports and the business courses
      they are taking.

I would like to upbraid these caballeros,
      to tell them something
about the sweetness of sexual love
      and the cruelty of words,
also the foolishness
      of thinking of women
in terms of conquest
      or cost efficiency
and how, in fact,
      the most improbable romances

are often the best.
      Suppose, for example,
that Virginia Woolf
      were to marry
what's his name—Rilke!
      King of the unreconciled polarity!

"Say to the still earth, I flow!
        Say to the rapid water, I am!"
Now that's fine writing.
        Then there's *Mrs. Dalloway*

and those other great novels:
        resonant forms, resonant forms!
Virginia, Virginia,
        you're my favorite Virginia.
You're Virginia Rilke now,
        the boys would say,
and I am a foolish fellow
        if I imagine
for a minute that Woolf,
        with her spells
of incapacitating and,
        at times, suicidal depression,
would make a suitable helpmeet
        for such a one as Rilke,
for whom the claims of marriage
        or indeed of any
demanding emotional relationship
        were irreconcilable
with his poetic vocation.
        To which I fancy myself replying,

Hoity toity, knaves—
        neither Leonard Woolf
not the sculptress Clara Westhoff
        were exactly what the doctor ordered

131

for Virginia and what's-his-name respectively,
         so why not each other
for each other?
         They would have been kind,
sweet, nervous, at least
         intermittently passionate,

and, in the long run,
         doomed, as who is not?
But during their time together
         they would have taken any number
of long, almost certainly stormy walks
         yet agreed that in each of us
the urge to be bad is strong
         and that love at its best
is often funny-strange
         and always funny-ha-ha.

ODE TO LANGUOR

My father and I are watching the opera *Susannah*,
            or at least I am, for my father has fallen
into a deep and dreamless slumber, the way

he always has—when I was young, he used
            to take me to the National Geographic Film
series on Wednesdays, and once,

as the Mud Men of New Guinea were shaking
            their spears at the camera, Johnny Taylor
(I was too self-conscious to sit with

anyone not my age) nudged me and said,
            "Look at that old man sleeping!" Forty
years later, I am almost an old man myself

and grateful for the quality of languor,
            almost certainly genetically transmitted.
Blessed parent! He is also the perfect

erotic role model, i.e., not. My father
            chased no skirts—after a while,
not even my mother's. When I think of

friends who have broken their hearts
            in the pursuit of unattainable women,
I am all the more grateful to my drowsy father.

Keats praised languor: easeful death was something
       he was more than half in love with,
though he didn't mean a passing like his own.

Keats wanted a death-in-art, a rich death,
       with a nightingale pouring forth its soul
as Susannah, wronged by the lustful elders,

pours forth hers, my eyes closing,
       my head bending toward that
of my dreamless father, this good man sleeping.

EL LIBRO DE BUEN AMOR

Here's how my mother taught me to dance;
      also, how she saved me from some bad whores—I mean, cops!
Well, I don't know what they were. It happened this way:
      I am standing outside my motel in the Buckhead region
of Atlanta, waiting, as the song says, not on a lady
      but on a friend, having discussed the Tyson-Ruddock fight
ad nauseam with my man Darryl the security guard

and even making a small bet, when a van pulls up
      and the two young women inside motion me over.
Would I like a date? they ask. Date, I reply, date?
      No, thanks, no dates, not tonight, I say,
as polite as my mother always taught me to be to everybody,
      yet curious, eager, even, to find out more
about such women and their "dates," so I start

to stick my head in their window and chat them up
      when I hear a voice say, "Don't do it, darling—they're cops!"
And there, on the balcony, between the ice maker
      and the soft drink machine, glowing fluorescently
and hovering maybe six inches off the ground,
      is an elderly woman, *very* familiar, hands raised in warning.
I'm staring, you bet, and thinking, cops?

I see the bad men of Atlanta suspended by their testicles
      from the streetlights like the crucified slaves
in *Spartacus* who line the road to Rome. . . .
      Just then my man Darryl appears to collect on the wager,

but he, too, freezes, transfixed by the eldritch vision;
        his eyes bug out of his head as he stammers, "It is
thy m-m-mother's spirit; / Doomed for a certain term to walk

the night, and for the day confined to fast in fires . . . ,"
        but I interrupt because it really is my mother,
or at least that aspect of her which is alive in me
        and looks out for my best interests,
the part that has me dancing just beyond the reach
        of *les filles de joie* and those cops as well,
my pelvis juking now, my hips swivelling skinny and fast.

I shake my money-maker, I shimmy and slide;
        tearing away from bug-eyed Darryl, I samba down Piedmont
as the bubbas of Buckhead rush from their lairs to cry,
        "Go, man, go!" and "Don't he dance good!"
I dance to defy the whores and the crummy cops, too,
        my fanny pumping left and right as they claw at me,
their hoarse howls splitting the air over Atlanta,

but mainly I am dancing for that wise woman
        my mother who, when I was born, wrapped me in a blanket
first thing and fed me and then wrote my name
        in the Book of Good Love—to her,
the daughters of joy are hapless, to be sure,
        but those cops are something else altogether,
i. e., abandoned by God.

LA FORZA DEL DESTINO IN THE TRI-STATE AREA

As I sit here listening to Verdi's opera,
which is one of his lesser ones
but a pretty good piece of work
no matter what the critics say,
I realize that I am going to spend
the rest of my life
in the Tri-State Area,
by which I mean not Florida, Georgia, and Alabama
or even New York, New Jersey, and Connecticut

but that combination of moods and ideas
in which childhood memories overlap
with the things I am doing at present
as well as whatever it is I am reading.
I feel so strongly about this
that I would say it's my destiny right now
to be thinking of the time
my parents took me to visit some friends
who lived below a couple named Fox,

and that even though I was old enough to know better,
still, I was more than a little anxious
about meeting those neighbors on the stairs
in their old-fashioned clothes,
eyes bulging slightly,
tongues hanging out like red neckties,
smiles more like leers than smiles;
should I pat their noses
or offer them some of my candy?

And while I am thinking
about how foolish I was as a child,
I am also planning to meet these same parents of mine
at the Grand Hotel in Point Clear, Alabama,
which I imagine to be an old, rather formal establishment
with a restaurant where they serve very good food,
and as I pack my bag,
I think about and pack as well my copy
of a book about different aspects of neurophysiology,

which is the kind of witty yet sensitive study
I would like to write myself someday.
Anyway, that is why I no longer have a foot
in both camps or agree that there are two sides
to any question or that every game is a toss-up
or that it takes only two to tango.
Freud was right: our lives aren't determined,
they're overdetermined,
and since that is how they are going to be

no matter how we feel about them,
maybe we should try to think nice
or at least interesting thoughts all the time
and be kind to the parents
who gave us our lives in the first place
and read books that will make us
not only smarter but more fun to be around.
Oh, and listen to as much music as possible:
the more forza, the better the destino.

PORTRAIT OF THE ARTIST'S PARENTS AS YOUNG DOGS

The home where my mother lives is full of women
who say they've "lost" their husbands,
as though the men managed to squeeze under a fence
or dart through a gate someone had left open.
Now they won't come when called,
and my own mother will have to phone
the Humane Society to say,

Have you seen my husband, a quiet man,
affectionate though not demonstrative?
The night before he died, my father asked my mother
if there was any money left, and when she said there was,
he said let's get out of this place;
when she answered that he couldn't walk
and she couldn't see, he said that's all right,

we'll manage, let's just go.
Since then she says nothing seems real anymore
and sometimes she says she wants to be where he is now,
though not dead, surely,
and not in that awful hospital
where she saw him last,
where she calls for the nurse and says,

When I touch his face, I can't feel anything,
I don't think he's breathing anymore;
the nurse says, He's not,
and *a couple of terriers slip through the door*

and break for the open. They race, tumble,
spring up, nip each other's flanks,
tear across a sunny meadow together toward a dark wood.

A FLACCID PENIS

It sows not, neither does it reap.
And the one to whom it does not respond
calls it impotent, as though
it should not discriminate,
should go where it's told,
do as it is commanded.

If that were so,
its owner would be a happier man.
Yet the flaccid penis itself is not unhappy,
is not dissatisfied with its appearance,
thinks of itself not as loathsome
because unmanly, unengorged, unred

but modest and unassuming, pink as a girl,
as well out of it
in its musky tent
as a heroine dreaming
of a cool bath in a marble tank,
in a darkened chamber, in a hot land.

THE FIRST LOVERS

They didn't know what to do or how to do it,
but they talked it over as best they could:
pointing, smiling, showing their empty hands,
then windmilling their arms wildly

in anticipation of the unknowable,
the thing that would soon be theirs.
He had seen the baboons do it
and had even tried it with them once,

but the baboons wouldn't have him;
they chittered and puffed their chests
and then surged upward, the whole herd together,
disappeared like a wave into the trees.

And she had watched the fish and wondered
if it were harder for them because they had no legs
or easier since they were smooth all over and lacked parts,
at least parts that she could see.

They knew it was right when everything fit, above
as well as below. It took a while to work out the rhythm,
and once they stopped to check each other's hands again
to make sure they were still empty.

It wasn't much fun.
They were so excited and unsure of themselves
that they felt like the twins they had seen one day,
the one who was identical

and the one who didn't resemble anyone at all.
So that as they lay sleeping in each other's arms,
they dreamed of other sweethearts,
good ones this time, patient, more experienced.

And then they dreamed of us. We frightened them:
in their dreams we were taller than they were
and lightly haired. How ugly we were!
And how unhappy, because we weren't like them at all,

and everything we did was different, wrong.
The first lovers turned uneasily in their sleep,
and as they turned, they ate the meat of forgetfulness.
And when they woke, they didn't recognize themselves,

much less each other. And then they realized
what they had become: that they were the same
as they'd had always been, unavoidably,
but now they were new people as well, adorable strangers.

That was how the race began. And language:
sounds ballooned out of their mouths, risible at first,
then affecting. They composed songs for each other,
and poems, plays, thick squarish novels.

But they liked the old gestures best:
the smiles, the little caresses, the open hands
which still say, My life before I met you
was like this, it was this way, it was nothing.

THE FIRST TAX COLLECTOR

They couldn't figure out who he was or what he wanted
or why he wanted it from them—why not another village

where the hunt had been more successful
or some hamlet where the crops had come in big-time?

Why them with their greasy pots and their little handfuls
of roots and berries, not even picked over yet?

He kept smiling and said that everyone had to pay
and that the money wasn't for him, it was for his boss,

the king. King? said the people. King, king!
he said, the guy who lives behind that hill there,

and the tax collector jerked his thumb over his shoulder.
But the people still wanted to know why and he got mad

and said it was to pay for the things
they couldn't do themselves and they said like what

and he looked distracted for a minute and said
well, like collect taxes and they said Oh, listen,

we tax ourselves all the time. We've given up so much
already, they said, you don't know the half of it.

First, each of us has suffered an irreversible loss;
it happened when we were born or just after.

Then every morning it's something else, and we end up
starving that we might eat, thirsting that we might drink:

the day breaks, things look pretty good, and then it's
starve, thirst, work for play that comes late, if ever.

And that's our lives. Yet out of affection,
out of good will, we make gestures of normalcy every day:

we vote, we marry, we have children, we join the PTA,
we keep our homes in good repair,

all the while thinking the whole deal faintly comical.
We *persist*, is the main thing. And now you want more?

Forget it, we won't be paying your taxes.
And the tax collector looked annoyed and said

Listen, you don't want me to whistle up my boys, do you?
He said you'll get used to it; the folks over in Bramble did,

and the ones in Rocktown are starting to see things our way.
But the people had heard enough, so they took the tax man out

and put him in a well. Then they coined the word "emissary."
Then they sent emissaries to Bramble and Rocktown

and encouraged them not to listen, not to pay.
And the king didn't get any taxes that year.

The following year, there was no king.
Yet the people taxed themselves and put a good face on it,

and after a while they began to wonder what it would be like
to give up everything. There would be nothing left

but their names and the names of the towns they lived in
and, after a while, not even that.

The people would live the way the animals do:
empty, naked, quiet, poor.

So they did it. They gave it all away,
all except the one thing that comforted them the most

when they couldn't feed themselves or were so filthy
that the dirt felt like their own skin.

We have to hang on to something! said one old man,
and some of the young rowdies agreed with him.

Then punches were thrown, the miller's nose was bloodied,
and almost everyone said something they didn't really believe.

But a woman, speaking softly, explained what
they all knew to be true, so that the old man was persuaded,

and while the young rowdies grumbled, finally they too said
Yeah, it would be best if there were nothing left,

not even the resentment they'd all wrapped themselves in
on cold nights or bitten savagely

like a piece of bread someone might find
at the bottom of a sack she'd sworn was empty.

LITTLE STABS OF HAPPINESS

The night Sam Cooke was shot,
I ran out into the back yard
and shouted, "Suck my dick, God!"
My father slapped my face,
said if he ever heard me
say anything like that again,
I could forget about driving, ever—
I'd be in my own house
with my own kids
and he'd show up
to take away the car keys.
Like I cared:
Sam Cooke was dead.

Every time I hear Sam Cooke's voice
on the radio, I feel these little stabs
of happiness, then a grief so profound
I've had to pull over to the side
of the road and gasp for breath,
my face in my hands
like Jerome in his hermit's cave
after Alaric sacked Rome
and "the light had gone out of the world."
Poor me! The knives of joy slash and chop.
There's nowhere to go,
my car's too small,
yet I'm happy!
Crowded and happy!

And miserable also.
Sam Cooke, you send me,
honest you do.

The Gigolo in the Gazebo

There is a gigolo in the gazebo, Mother,
worrying about the weather:
someone was buried in the base of the gazebo,
and now a cloud is passing over the moon,
and rain may wash away the flagstones and cement,
said to be poorly mixed, leaving the gigolo
with a body and no alibi, since Mrs. Alfred Uruguay
will never admit to having been with him
in the boudoir or even the foyer, much less the gazebo.

Mrs. Alfred Uruguay thinks the gigolo fancies himself
and is fearful of indiscretion; she doesn't know
he is so distracted that he can't decide
whether to relight his cheroot or take out another.
Now he smooths his brillantined hair and pauses—
was it he who put the body in the base of the gazebo?
And what to do with his hands? In the parlor,
he could wipe them on any antimacassar,
but now he is alone in the gazebo. Solo,

the gigolo would like to have a split of Veuve Cliquot
sent 'round. He wishes he were a thinking stone
or one of the first white men in the mountains
of New Guinea so that he could make the natives cry,
"Here comes the man from heaven in his evening clothes,
his boiled shirt!" The gigolo wishes someone would
land in, not just any biplane, but a De Haviland Foxmoth
to take him away from Mrs. Alfred Uruguay and from
his present ennui and away from the body under the gazebo.

BOTTOMLESS CUP

The best thing in the world is coffee,
especially the cup I have first thing
every day, three scoops of espresso
and one of American coffee with chicory,
filtered. Around town it's commercially
prepared and lousy, but I drink it anyway
in honor of that first cup, which makes
the subsequent ones not so bad,
and because I love the stuff.
Of course various hosts and hostesses
in this city make very serviceable coffee
after the dinners to which I am often
invited, having something of a reputation
as a useful hand in the kitchen
and more than passable conversationalist,
but by then it's too late in the evening
for good coffee, which only disturbs sleep,
thus dulling one's appreciation
of that matutinal cup, the first one,
every day! It's silly to get caught up
in rituals, I know, but a friend told me
his father recovered from his mother's death
by taking up again the little routines
he'd practiced daily, all his life.
So coffee might save me from despair
one of these days, since I certainly
don't expect to go through

without my share of blows. Well, you see,
that ruins it; now all this coffee-drinking
has a purpose, which it shouldn't.
I don't even need the stuff to wake up with,
being fairly jumpy most of the time anyway.
I suppose I drink it because I want
to be more like coffee myself,
the thing people need when they get up
in the morning and then all day long,
something even the poor can afford.
I want to find myself everywhere.
I want to be the thing that's bad for you
if you get too much.

THE FLESH EATERS

I came across another people who were anthropophagous: the ugliness of their features says so.

C. Colón, *Textos y documentos completos*

1   *The Crew, With Less Fear Than Wonder*

> A race of ugly folk without heads
> who have eyes in each shoulder,
> headless people with mouths and noses
> on their backs, ugly fellows
> with upper lips so big that when
> they sleep in the sun they cover
> all their faces with it,
> a race whose ears hang down
> to the ground, hermaphroditos
> whose male side begets children
> and whose female side bears them,
> a people with a single foot
> that shades them when they lie
> on their backs, a people who live on
> the smell of one kind of apple,
> and if they have not that smell,
> they die: these things were written of
> by good Sir John Mandeville
> in his celebrated *Travels*.

2   *Chipangu, A Large Island of the East Described by Marco Polo and Later Called Japan*

               Hum, hey!
Hum!
                         Messer Colón!   can it be
The Great Khan   there he is!   hey
                                       This way!
            No, no—this way!

3   *Fernando, Son of the Very Magnificent Lord Don Cristobal Colón, Grand Admiral of the Ocean Sea*

In his youth my father was a mariner but also a madcap, pause. Once a Genoese merchant fleet in which he sailed was attacked by a pirate called Coullon the Elder. The slaughter was terrible: men threw themselves into the waves rather than suffer the pain of their wounds. Pause, pause. My father's ship burned to the waterline and he swam six miles to shore; when he crawled onto the beach, he was a new man. As he regained his health, he conceived of a plan to get gold from the Great Khan written of by Marco Polo and raise armies to take back the Holy Sepulchre from the Saracens. Pause. He seldom smiled after that day.

4   *The Ancient Cartographers on the Presence of Hippo-griffs and Anthropophagi on the Borders of Their Maps*

Where you know nothing, place terrors.

5   *Fernando, Son of, Etc.*

On the evening of September 25th, 1492, Martin Pinzón shouted from the poop of the *Pinta* that he had sighted Chipangu, but the next day the sea was empty. Pause. The three ships finally touched land, but my father kept searching for Chipangu, which the natives called Colba, then Caniba, then Ciabo, pause. My father did considerable naming of islands himself, often changing them to accord with a name used by Marco Polo, so that Yamaye, for instance, became Yanahica. Some of the men said that the great discoverer was not fond of discovery.

6   *Anacaona, A Carib Woman of Exceptional Beauty*

> One of Colón's lieutenants
> tried to have his way with me
> but I treated him so with my nails
> that he wished he had never begun.
>
> Then he took a piece of rope
> and whipped me so soundly
> that I came to terms with him
> to save myself from death.

Later he told the others
I was so lively
he would have thought
I had been brought up

in a school for whores,
but even as I gave myself
I bit and scratched and twisted,
for I was fighting him.

7   *Fernando the Son*

Pause. In his later voyages my father's distemper was even
more pronounced. He went for thirty-two nights without sleep one
time and imagined himself in a sea white as milk with three figures
walking toward him across the water, emissaries of the Great
Khan. Another day he decided that the sea had disappeared and
that his boats were sailing through a colossal field of yellow corn.
Once he thought he was in Paradise, pause. Yet always he sought
Chipangu.

8   *The Crew, With As Much Fear As Wonder This Time*

It rained. It rained.
Yet a strange fire surrounded us.
And a waterspout came down
from the sky to cast us about

like toothpicks. But the Admiral
read from the Gospel of St. John
and traced crosses in the sky
with his sword while the waters
grew still and the sky quiet.

9   *Chipangu, With Unmistakable Irony*

Hum, hum!   Messer Colón!
            Over here, Messer Colón!   This way
     to the gold   good Messer
                    gold for blue beads!   Hum!
Oh, the greedy Moor!
            Oh   hum   the nasty, greedy grabber!

10   *Fernando*

Once some men were brought to camp with pieces of flesh
missing from their bodies, and my father was given to understand
that cannibals had eaten mouthfuls of them, though he did not
believe this. Yet something had torn away the skin and muscle of
these creatures—what? The Admiral died repentant of much that
he had done, though he was not dishonored. Pause. Not wholly
dishonored. Pause, pause. Not in Valladolid.

THE BIRTH AND UNTIMELY DEATH
OF THE MUSICAL LEGACY OF THE OUTLAW JESSE JAMES

Carl Sandburg's immigrant father worked six days
      a week as a blacksmith's helper for fourteen cents
an hour and spent everything he earned
      on his family except for the occasional nickel
he gave to a street musician who'd sing the ballad
      of Jesse James. August Sandburg would request

"de Yesse Yames song" and drop his coin
      in the guy's cup. The singer'd torture his instrument
for a minute, then: some people say he crazy,
      some people say he insane. A-whoo gawd,
some people say the singer crazy, some say
      he insane. But he don't care about

nothin' (have mercy) 'cept that old Jesse James.
      Hot damn! August Sandburg's been zapped
by the music's wounding joy. He throws
      his cap down and "cuts loose" right there
on the Galesburg sidewalk; wagging his calloused
      forefingers in the air, he shouts, "De beauty's

still on duty, y'all! De beauty's still on duty!"
      Because Jesse James was nobody's fool
and nobody's helper; he was his own boss
      and set his own wages. He was the first rock star,
like Elvis, only earlier and less fake.
      Imagine JFK in the months before he killed himself;

it's the summer of 1963, and he's lying
    on the White House floor thinking about
the Yesse Yames song and sharing a little reefer
    with one of Sam Giancana's tomatoes,
and that darned Caroline, cute as a puppy
    yet always fooling with the dial,

has left the radio tuned to one
    of those freaky rock stations. JFK hears the drums
on Bobby Freeman's "Do You Wanna Dance";
    they sound like somebody slapping
a wet cardboard box with an ax handle,
    and suddenly he's zapped, too;

he's prissing around like August Sandburg,
    he's writhing like Henry Adams before the dynamo
in the Gallery of Machines at the Great
    Exposition of 1900, "historical neck broken
by the sudden irruption of forces totally new."
    JFK gets up and he thinks, Fuck Sinatra

and he says, "I want to hear the Yesse Yames song"
    or he wants to be the singer of the Yesse Yames song
or be Yesse Yames himself. I'll fix Castro's ass
    once I'm the outlaw Yesse Yames, you betcha!
Or maybe you fixed it already, jefe:
    sometimes it's hard to remember

if you did what you did or if you just got it
        mixed up with all the songs you've ever heard.
Now it's November 22—crawling past
        the Texas Book Depository, the limo driver
is looking for some good tunes but accidentally
        dials up Elvis singing "Bossa Nova Baby,"

recorded earlier that same year;
        JFK grabs the Secret Service guy's gun
and shoots himself in the head rather than go on living
        in a world that plays such crappy music.
Elvis kills the president! Elvis goes to jail!
        Elvis needs to go to jail anyway

for selling out August Sandburg,
        for betraying Yesse Yames,
and for killing off rock and roll itself
        nine years earlier, in December 1954,
raw power turning to Vegas horsecrap in the
        false start to "Milkcow Blues Boogie,"

where he says, "Hold it, fellas. That don't move.
        Let's get real, real gone." But future president
Richard M. Nixon will need Elvis as a kiss-ass stoolie
        during his own administration, so he pays
phony desperado Lee Oswald to take the fall,
        what a chump.

YOUR FAMOUS STORY

The table has been cleared,
and the guests are sitting around the fire

with glasses of brandy and chartreuse
as you begin to tell your famous story:

how you and your wife were desperate
to go somewhere, anywhere, after the birth

of your first child and finally found
a service in the yellow pages, a church group

that would send a babysitter, a gentlewoman,
a grandmotherly type who came highly recommended,

someone who had raised children of her own.
You went to a movie and a coffeehouse

and when you got back, the sitter was
just as you had left her, calm and smiling,

assuring you that everything had been fine,
that your little girl was an angel,

and you laughed, saying that she must not have
changed the baby's diapers or she would have seen

it was a boy. The sitter looked at the wall
and said in a voice you had never heard before

that while the baby might have been a boy
when you left, he was certainly a girl now.

You dashed upstairs and tore off the baby's pajamas
but of course he was fine, and that evening

you told your story for the first time to the police
and then, next morning, the church group.

They hid nothing, said the sitter had a history
of threatening children with knives,

but they were told all that was in the past,
and now the good liberal churchwomen were trying

to rehabilitate her with lay counseling
and the offer of regular work.

There was a hearing, and you told your story again.
The babysitter went behind walls.

Your son grew up healthy and strong,
and now he dines out

on the story you are telling us now,
the night coming down around your house

like a hand that closes around the heart,
opens a little, never lets go.

Hunka Hunka Amor Caliente

Almost everyone I know has a secret life.
In most cases "secret" means "sexual,"
also "mental."
The general feeling seems to be that
we are all corpses on vacation,
therefore why not have two lives
and twice as much fun
before you have to jump back into that box?

However, "mental" does not mean easy.
Prostitutes say,
with respect to their customers,
"Even the nice ones aren't nice."
Therefore you have to be nice
but smart as well,
which probably means
avoiding prostitutes,

most of whom have awful expressions
on their faces, as though
they want to jump back into that box immediately.
I am an Ecclesiastes 8:15 man myself,
wherein it says, "A man hath no better thing
under the sun, than to eat, and to drink,
and to be merry," otherwise he jumpeth into that box
feeling a certain chagrin
and not the chagrin d'amour, either.

Same authority, chapter 9, verse 4:
"A living dog is better than a dead lion."
Your dog is not nice, though.
Your dog is nasty.
Too, your dog has to jump back into that box
a lot sooner than we do;
hence, no secret life for it.

For the rest of us
it's be nice, be smart,
get mental,
then back into that box
and zoom, off to the undiscovered country.

A POOR UNHAPPY WRETCHED SICK MISERABLE LITTLE FRENCH BOY

A little motherless French schoolboy
is traveling across America with his father,
and when they get to Reno,
the dad asks the boy if he would mind
his bringing a woman to their room
and the boy, who has a bad cold
from all of the air conditioning in America,

says yes, he would mind,
that it would make him feel funny,
and when the father says,
what do you mean, feel funny,
the little wretch says
he doesn't know what he means
and crosses and uncrosses his skinny white legs

and blows his nose into a big French handkerchief.
I too have felt funny without knowing why,
as when my boss says,
Could you step into my office a moment,
I'd like to have a word with you,
and I want to say I'd rather not,
it would make me feel funny,

or when my wife tells me she wants to have
a serious talk with me this evening
after I get home from work,

and I want to say, Oh, darling, let's not talk!
I'd feel funny if we were to talk!
At times like this,
I am the boy with the bad haircut,

the one in the cheap blazer and short pants,
my books in a strap the priests will take
to my nervous matchstick legs
if I stumble over my *verbes irrégulières.*
I am turning into
a poor unhappy wretched sick miserable little French boy,
and the world is my angry, faithless father.

THE PHYSICS OF HEAVEN

Everyone will be there at once:
your husbands and boyfriends
in their relation to you

as the wife and sweetheart of each
but also in equivalent if not identical relationships
with their other wives and sweethearts:

Harry, Edward and Maurice will coexist peacefully
with themselves and with you
but also with Sheila, Nancy, Kim, and so on

and all at the same time. And you, you'll be all
your happy selves: a little girl, a big girl, a woman,
a baby, everything except dead. And the pets!

Here's Beowulf, who died under the wheels of a milk truck,
running and playing again! And Matilda,
who chased you around the porch when she had distemper,

wagging her tail now as she licks your hand.
And all the fish who died before you could give them names,
though you meant to. And both hamsters.

And your parents, but this time they love each other,
which is to say they love themselves, love you.
It doesn't make sense. But no one notices, so it makes sense.

THE PHYSICS OF HELL

No one you want to be here, is—
but the boy you invited to your twelfth birthday,
the one who called you that morning

and said he had a cold, even though
everyone else had seen him the night before
at the football game, running and laughing,

he's here—you were the only one without a date
at your own party because he wasn't there,
but he's here, smirking, empty-handed.

And the others, all the guys you'd broken up with,
they're here, too, with all the other girls
they've shamed and maddened, quarreling,

the din unbearable. It's the worst of times
and the worst of times. The friends who bored you
and then broke with you because you weren't interesting

are here, and so are the pets you starved,
the ones you let run in the street,
whose tails you pinched in the doors of their cages.

And you, you act selfish, break hearts—
you do what everyone else does, because hell makes sense.
But no one notices, so it doesn't make sense.

Nosebleed, Gold Digger, KGB, Henry James, Handshake

Here's the thing: you're coming out of the men's room
and you run into someone you work with and he says

Hi, how's it going and you say Fine, you?
and he says Great and you go to your office

and he goes to the men's room and then
you run into him again on your way back,

only this time you say nothing to him and vice versa.
Is that because you don't have to or because

you don't want to? Nothing has changed
in those few minutes, surely, but perhaps you should ask

and he should, too, because what if he had a nosebleed
in the men's room and needs to hear you say

That's nothing, happens to me all the time
or Here's the number of a good doctor?

Or say you got the bad phone call from your wife
who says That's it, you creep, I'm out of here,

giving this colleague the chance to say
You can get her back, give her this big ring,

or I always thought she was a cheap gold digger,
better luck next time. We could check on

each other constantly, of course, but that
would lead to crazy stuff, calling up in the middle

of the night to see if the other person is sleeping
or walking in on someone else's big sexy interlude

and saying Whew, you're doing great, thank god.
So let this poem be my signal to each of you

that I am thinking of you all the time;
if you're reading this, I'm looking out for you,

kind of: if you visited Russia in the old days,
the KGB would assign you a "minder" so you wouldn't steal

any state secrets but also to help you
if you got lost, and frankly, I'd rather be lost.

Also, what secret could the state have
that could possibly interest any right-minded person?

Be kind, be kind, be kind, said Henry James,
but that was easy for him to say, since he spent

most of his life alone. Nameless colleague,
I salute you and set down herewith my best wishes

for a *bonne continuation*: I shake your hand!
And you hers, and she his, and so on.

LATER UNCOLLECTED POEMS

The Wedding Vows

Do you promise to love, honor, cherish?
To do all the talking as he just sits there,
            furious about his job? As her jaw works
like the drive gear on a Singer sewing machine?
        As he lurches through the door every Saturday
with a bag of clubs on his shoulder?

        As he comes home tired and sunburned
and finds her naked on the kitchen floor,
            an empty bottle of cooking sherry
by her side and a wad of chocolate
        stuck to her face because she was too drunk
to get it in her mouth?

        As he taps a total stranger on the shoulder
at the theater and asks if the actor
            on stage is a boy or a girl,
and when the guy looks at him open-mouthed
        and finally hisses, "Be quiet,"
tells the guy to mind his own business?

        As she finally agrees to go
to the company softball game
            but sits with the other team because
"the light is better there,"
        and the novel she pulls out is not only
hardback but in another language?

As he says if she wants kids, fine,
but they'll be her responsibility?
        As she goes through the buffet line
a fourth time? As he goes through
    only three times but stacks everything
on his plate at once:

    meat loaf, king mackerel, spinach pie,
egg roll, potatoes au gratin, canned peaches,
        cottage cheese, crispy-fried noodles,
cole slaw, brownie? As she starts out
    a porcelain-cheeked girl painted by Fragonard
and ends up a second baseman?

    As he stumbles through the mall,
face a mask, belly hanging over
        the waistband of his beltless pants,
pausing in the food court to wheeze
    that he needs a "senior Coke"?
As she says "What? What?"

    As he tells the waitress
nobody can read the damned menu?
        As her hands shake? As he rises from the chair
and falls back and looks up, scared?
    As she says they've got to sell the car?
As he goes into the hospital

    and doesn't come out and doesn't come out?
As she can't sleep anymore?

As he can't wake up? After all this,
do you promise to love, honor, cherish—
        do you? You do, you know you do.
This is why. These are the reasons.

The End of Poetry

"Does anyone fuck or die?"
—television producer asking a writer about his script

That year, we all fucked.
    None of us died,
        though one of us hated her husband so much
she threatened to bite him to death.
    But even they fucked;
        with those two,
it was fight and fuck, fight and fuck,
    every night and all weekend.
        And the rest of us fucked, too,
or fucked as much as our partners would let us.

And then the dying began.
    To no one's surprise,
        it was less fun than the fucking.
Even when our enemies died,
    it was awful because it took so long:
        a quick death let us say
"she had it coming"
    or "it couldn't have happened to a nicer guy,"
        and then we'd regret our churlishness
and forget the whole affair.

But slow deaths made us think,
    and we didn't like that at all.
        That's the great thing about fucking:

you don't have to think,
       and you're never alone.
              These days we don't fuck or die
or even think as much as we used to.
      We just dream,
            sometimes by ourselves
but more often in groups so large

they fill meadows and stadiums and civic centers,
      all teeming with silent dreamers,
            the space around them lush with airy visions.
We're working on our dream syntax
      and we're getting better
            at our punctuation, too:
I find myself more and more capable
      of continuing a dream I like with commas
           or stopping a bad one
with a single, decisive period.

And though we don't fuck or think anymore,
      we still die, though we don't call it dying:
           we call it something else,
though no one remembers what,
      because we don't remember anymore, either.
           There is no more television,
and poetry is on the way out
      as more and more people become poets.
           We're grammarians now,
shaping the emptiness above us,

giving it form and texture,
    then tumbling up to meet it.
        We disappear over the ocean,
we circumnavigate—
    I love that word,
        which means to come back not as ourselves
but as animals, say, or books.
    Sorrow! we cry out as we laugh
        and wave to our friends, Beauty!
The air thickens around us, and we rise.

THE URGE TO BE BAD IS STRONG

and also ubiquitous in every historical period:
 it overtook Mark Twain when he described
Emerson, Longfellow, and Holmes as rascally blackguards
 in his Whittier birthday dinner speech
and nobody laughed except a single hysterical guest

whose name has not been handed down to infamy,
 and today it overtakes Dr. Henry Moffett
in the office next to mine as he makes yet another girl cry:
 "Didn't you *read* the assignment?" he asks,
then "Wasn't it in *English*?" and "Didn't you *understand* it?"

The girl cries and cries and answers as best she can:
 yes, she read it; yes, it was in English, kind of;
no, she didn't understand it, while, drunk with fury,
 Dr. Moffett says there is nothing he can do for her,
nothing anyone can do, as the girl sobs without respite,

but no one cares, and for a moment the world seems divided
 into sadists and their victims and the texts
they cannot agree on. But authors, it's not your fault,
 nor is it the fault of the poor girl
whose only crime is inexperience, nor is it even

the fault of Dr. Moffett, who has an excess of bile—
 indeed, in many ways, his lot is the sorriest,
for authors will continue to write their books,
 oblivious to popular and critical reception,
and surely the girl will grow in knowledge,

while Dr. Moffett will merely become each day
     more peevish and irritable.
Indeed, who has not this same urge overtaken?
     E. g., it overtook Bob Dylan when he accepted an award
from the Emergency Civil Liberties Committee

and took it upon himself to say, three weeks after JFK
     was killed, that he sympathized with Oswald.
And it overtook a woman of my acquaintance
     at a reception following a poetry reading
when she walked up to a perfect stranger

and said "Where did they get that poet?
     as she drew her finger across her neck,
not realizing that the poet himself, who had changed
     his shirt and removed his reading glasses,
was indeed her exasperated questionee.

And it has overtaken me more times
     than I can tell you: it's in the marrow
of each of the bones of my body, this urge,
     it's lodged in my throat like the chew-toy
that is brought to you by the dog

who shakes and shakes his head but won't let go.
     Emerson divided everything into the Me,
meaning the mind, the soul, the personality,
     and the Not-Me, which is everything else,
including the body, often beautiful to behold

yet surely dumb as dirt, not to mention spiteful.
    But then Emerson had no excess of bile,
for when Twain apologized, he asked who was this fellow,
    and what did he think he had done, the Sage of Concord
having about him a sublime forgetfulness,

especially in later years. Charming prospect:
    like Emerson, to view this nether world
with growing oblivion.
    Ah, but Dr. Moffett too is growing older!
Yet merely rebarbative.

STRANIERO

Ah, Florence! You have your art.
    You have your history. You have your medieval walls
and your Renaissance palazzi. You have
        your open-air markets and your leather goods shops.
           Mainly, though, you have your food: your *bistecche*,
        your *tortellini*, and so on, so that while
           I'm taking my students to see Dante's house,
I might walk by the restaurant
        I'll be dining at that very evening and think, Yum.

There is only one problem with dining out
        over there, and that's my name:
there is no "k" and no "y" in Italian,
        and my wife's name is Hamby,
           which is just as bad since there's no "h,"
        so often when I make a reservation
           I tell them my name is "Biondo,"
which means "blond," and when we get
        to the restaurant and the maître d' asks

for my name I say, "Biondo" and sometimes
        I hold up a lock of my hair and say, "See?
Biondo." But after a while I feel silly
        doing that, so sometimes I use a German name,
           since there are a lot of Germans in Tuscany,
        though once I reserved under the name
           "Pfeiffer," and the maître d' said,
"*Veramente*? *Come* Michelle Pfeiffer, *l'attrice*?"
        and I said, "*Si, come* Michelle,"

and when we got to the restaurant,
        the waiters ran over excitedly
and were terribly disappointed
        when they saw it was just us
                and not the celebrated actress
                and so they pouted the rest of the evening
                        and gave us lousy service,
and we were so embarrassed
        that we never went back.

Now you can spell out any name in Italian
        by using town names, sort of like the military alphabet
in which VC becomes Victor Charlie,
        and in that case "Kirby" would be Kursaal-Imola-
                Roma-Bologna-York, but not everyone understands that,
        and sometimes the guy who picks up the phone
                isn't the brightest person in the whole operation,
so I've tried this method too only to show up
        and have no record of any reservation at all.

Then I decided I would start making reservations
        under fairly common Italian names,
saying, for example, "Benelli,
        Gianni Benelli," and I start to spell it
                and they say, Nope, not necessary,
        see you at eight, Signor Benelli.
                Only once we wanted to go to Cibrèo,
arguably one of the three or four
        best restaurants in Italy,

so I called two weeks ahead and made
the reservation under the name of Viciani
or DiMicheli or Prati or something like that,
and on the appointed evening we set off for Cibrèo
and then stop to have an *aperitivo*, and while
we are in the bar, who should come by
but our friend Ernie, who is also teaching
in Florence, and so we have another drink,
and then when we get to the restaurant,

and the maître d' asks me for my name,
I'm standing there with my head fizzing,
thinking Bianchi? Galvani?
and Barbara is looking at me
as though I'm an idiot, and finally
the maître d' says, But who are you, signore?
which is a question that has a lot
of possible answers, though for the moment
all I can think to say is, I don't know,

but we're very hungry, can't you seat us anyway?
and he says, Of course, you're in Italy,
each of us must eat, and he seats us,
and we "eat like priests," as they say there,
though whenever he passes our table
the maître d' wriggles his eyebrows at me comically
and on the way out he says, Remember yet?
and we have a little laugh together,
though I'm not really amused.

And it's just a few days later
  that we are in Rome, where we eat at
l'Arancia dell'Oro and Archimede
  and Al Brigante Crocco and all these other
    great restaurants without problem because
  by now I'm back to the moronic yet efficent "Biondo,"
  and also we visit the Capitoline
and the Roman Forum and, most movingly (Barbara cries),
  the Protestant Cemetery, where we read:

    This Grave
   Contains all that was mortal,
     of a
    YOUNG ENGLISH POET,
     who,
   on his Death Bed,
  in the Bitterness of his Heart
at the malicious Power of His Enemies,
    Desired
these words to be engraved on his Tomb Stone
   Here Lies One
  Whose Name Was Writ in Water
    Feb. 24 1821

and by now we have exactly one more
  evening in Italy before we catch
our return flight to Tallahassee,
  so we decide to spend it at A'ddo' Masto,
    the pizzeria so renowned that there is always

a long line outside, and so once again
    I start to give my name—some name—to the maître d',
but he says, Nope, got it already, then scribbles
  something in his book and waves me away,

and naturally I am burning with curiosity
    to see what he has written, so finally I pretend
to go to the men's room so I can swing by
  the table with the book on it and see
    that where Kirby or Pfeiffer or Biondo
should be, he has put *straniero*,
    that is, foreigner, outsider, strange person,
and I think, Right, that's what
  I should have said to the other guy.

DIMITRI TIOMKIN, DIMITRI TIOMKIN

As a kid I loved Little Richard
and Chuck Berry, sure, but also
      Dimitri Tiomkin, whose name I repeated
to myself mantra-style because
      it was so mouth-filling and well-marbled,
especially within the Anglo-Vanilla context
      of "Ricky Nelson" and "John Wayne,"

and who left Russia
after the Revolution (there were
      not a lot of opportunities
for concert pianists just then)
      and made his way to Berlin, Paris, New York,
and, finally, Hollywood, where he ended up
      writing the scores for, among other films,

Red River, Rio Bravo, The Alamo,
The War Wagon, and *Giant,* and where
      he would turn his palms up and say
to a journalist, when asked how a Ukrainian
      could write music so lushly evocative
of the American West, "a steppe is a steppe
      is a steppe," and a cowboy like a cossack,

which was more than I, the consumer,
needed to know then—I mean,
      the images were the main thing,
of course, but with a Tiomkin score,

you always got more than your money's worth,
because that big lush sound always
helped you feel what the jaspers

and dudes and deputies and desperados on screen
were making you feel anyway,
although now that I understand more about composition
and opera and dramatic structure
and the humanities in general,
it occurs to me that the *High Noon*
theme does sound like a Mittel-European folk tune,

and therefore could not a balalaika
play it as well as the harp
and pizzicato strings that torment us
and Marshall Cooper and Miss Kelly
as we wait together for the train to bring
the killers to town and shoot
the outgunned lawman-slash-new husband to rags?

And does not the music for *Gunfight at
the OK Corral*, which movie moves as
inexorably toward a bloody finale as
any stage tragedy, reach all the way back
to the tenth century A. D., when priests
from the Eastern Empire were brought in
to teach Christianity, and Byzantine culture

began to saturate Russian with the alphabet,
the liturgical music, the literature of

the Greeks? And is not film critic
Charles Higham wildly fanning the old hog-leg
            yet hitting the bullseye every time
    when he describes *Duel in the Sun*, in which
            Jennifer Jones and Gregory Peck love

            and murder each other and die together
    as "a Wagnerian horse opera, a *Liebestod*
            among the cactus"? In the acceptance
speech for his third Oscar, Tiomkin,
            whose command of English was always
    a couple of bars behind his musical proficiency,
            said, "I like to thank Johannes Brahms,

            Johann Strauss, Richard Strauss, Richard Wagner,"
    and here everybody began to laugh, because
            a lot of people had made catty remarks
about film composers pilfering from
            the classics, and here was one of
    the great ones admitting it, "Beethoven,
            Rimsky-Korsakov," but by then he had

            to leave the stage because the
    laughter was too thunderous and he
            too dazed to continue, since
all he had wanted was to do what
            any true artist does and acknowledge
    his masters, so why was everybody laughing?
            Some other composers attacked Tiomkin

for giving away what only they
        still regarded as a trade secret,
                including Franz Waxman, himself
a gifted composer (*The Bride*
                of Frankenstein, Sunset Boulevard)
        yet one who took himself so seriously
                that all he could do was walk away

                sputtering after Tiomkin said,
        "I don't know why you're annoyed,
                Franz, I don't hear any influences of
these great composers in your music,"
        although you certainly could
        in Tiomkin's, because he crammed
                the movies with the music

                and the music with the notes,
        until both the one and the other
                were just as full to bursting
as any knock-, brat-,
                or blutwurst you've ever eaten
        since the days of your little-kid self
                sitting there with its popcorn

                and its Necco Wafers
        and its big red drink,
                the sound washing over and past,
history-quakes for the hard
                of hearing, ceiling-high tsunamis
        of musical goulash that left you
                with a dim glimmer of suspicion

that you couldn't have articulated—
not yet, at least—
about, not the so-called "pageant of human history,"
but the very life of the mind,
which, you find out later,
is like the movies themselves,
i. e., action-packed.

THE POSSUM BOYFRIEND

Often people say to me, "Dave,
    what does it sound like when you think?"
I tell them that mainly it sounds like harp music punctuated
    by car crashes and people screaming for their mama
but also the barely audible voice of Karl Marx
    depicting history as the hidden god in literature.

But even this is only partly true.
    The rest of the time I am simply recalling things
I have read or heard—for example,
    what my wife said to me when I left our house this evening.
A big fat possum has been trying to get into her office,
    a converted attic above our garage;

I have seen him climb the trellis and look into her window,
    and she says she has heard him coming to her office door,
his nails clicking on the stairs, then tumbling back down
    when she goes out to look at him.
So when I left the house, she said, "Don't be late—
    I might run off with my possum boyfriend."

And this makes me wonder: did women in earlier times
    refer to their possum boyfriends,
that is, did people back then think the way people do now?
    I think the answer might be yes, sort of,
that the patterns of thought are the same
    even if the specific words change.

For example, the phrase "possum boyfriend"
        reminds me of "robber bridegroom,"
because of the metrical equivalence
        but also because the ideas are the same:
forbidden love, eroticism heightened
        by the bizarre, and so on.

It's just that as a Post-Modern,
        my wife is allowed to be more ironic
and her signifiers to slip a little farther;
        thus "possum" instead of "robber"
and "boyfriend" instead of "bridegroom,"
        the element of play remaining constant.

When I get home, I am going to put my ear to my wife's head
        to see if I detect at least a possum in there
if not one of its more *recherché* relatives—
        the gibbon, the howler monkey, anything—
for without possums or the memory of possums
        our thoughts would be as sneezes, meaningless and loud.

ON BEING A POET

I am sitting in my office when the phone rings,
     and it's a colleague I know vaguely,
a home economics professor who has chaired
     a couple of committees I've been on, and she says,
"I'm going to be in your poetry workshop this term,
     David, what are we going to be doing in there?"
and for a moment I'm gulping for air like a guppie,

and then I regain my composure and say,
     "Mary, that's a permission-only course, I'll have
to look at some of your work before I say yes,"
     and suddenly she's the Jessica Walter character
in *Play Misty for Me*, only instead of going over
     to Clint Eastwood's house and slicing
his jungle-pattern '70s polyester shirts to shreds,

she's telling me I'm arrogant, I'm a snob,
     I think I'm better than other people
whereas I'm the one with no compassion,
     no compunction, no class, and then she concludes
by saying, "I will continue to write, David!"
     and I say, "So who's stopping you?" but by that time
she has already banged the phone down,

and I'm in a state, an absolute state,
     because I keep forgetting that all you have to do
is say the word "poet" to some people
     and they start projecting the strangest attitudes,

though the only time I was actually ever scorned
        for being a poet was when I was trying
to buy a house, and the negotiations fell through,

and the seller got angry and said,
        "You're a poet, aren't you?"
and I admitted I was, knowing something terrible
        was coming next, though what he said
was no worse than that I should go back
        to my poems and leave the cold, hard world of business
to men like himself, real men, practical types

who understand how things work,
        but I figured that I knew how things worked
in his case, at least, and that he was the kind
        of guy who thinks his wife is ugly
and his kids are dumb, the kind who sits next to me
        on airplanes and says, "Is there any *money* in that?"
after I confess my little secret,

though I think most of the businessmen
        I meet on planes are indifferent to
rather than scornful of my chosen profession,
        so that even though they often feel obliged
to wonder out loud why "poetry doesn't rhyme anymore,"
        before I am very far into my answer,
the poor devils have already drifted back to their laptops

or the in-flight movie, sorry they ever asked.
        But believe me, indifference and even scorn are better

than this assumed intimacy that turns to clawing
        and spitting rage when it's rebuffed, and right now
I'm wondering if this Mary woman is going to show up
        on my doorstep with a pistol, the way
one student did who said she was going

to kill herself unless I "fulfilled her needs,"
        whatever they were, or with a dead squirrel,
as the student did who said I'd had a number
        of past lives and the squirrel had been one of them,
or with a blood-soaked suicide note, like the one
        who said I had driven her crazy by talking to her
over the PA system when she went to the supermarket.

At a party once I introduced myself to a man
        I didn't know who said he sure knew me
because he was the director of the counseling center
        on campus and that his files were full of references
to Kirby the poet, and I said you're kidding,
        and he said no, in fact it was pretty typical
for certain kinds of people to assume an intimacy

with poets, since poets deal in hidden meanings.
        So unless you change your job, he went on,
you're always going to have certain people
        reading your poems and finding messages in them
that aren't really there, and I was stunned,
        I went over to the buffet table and got some more brie
and some grapes, but later that night

after I'd gone home, while I felt sorry
  for the poor disturbed people—I had to put up
with one of them every couple of years or so,
  but then they had to put up with themselves
twenty-four hours a day—I figured,
  as far as the messages go that either are or aren't
in the poems, really, who am I to say?

THE POTATO MASH (MORE INDEFINITE AND MORE SOLUBLE)

If Debussy had written the score to the story of my adolescence,
he would have called it, after the name of the poem
        by his good friend Mallarmé, *L'Après-Midi d'un Dope*.
So many adventures! All of them stupid.
    For a while I worked for a rock band;
I handled the bookings, the equipment, and the snacks.
        The band leader played the French horn,
which is all he knew how to play;
        it was the only rock and roll French horn in the business.

And the bassist, who had never played at all,
just hit whatever notes he felt like hitting,
        saying it didn't make any difference
because nobody ever paid any attention to the bass line anyway.
    Then there were the two blind brothers,
a drummer and a guitarist,
        good musicians who drank bourbon and ate doughnuts
during the shows, always with disastrous results,
        though the band was horrible to begin with.

We never accomplished our goal of meeting pliant women,
and everywhere we went,
        the drunken fishermen we played for were mad at us
because our music had not brought out any women for them.
    Instead we played songs like "The Mashed Potatoes,"
each time to a smaller and surlier crowd.
        We "loosened classical tonality" the way Debussy did,
and at times we destroyed it, like Schoenberg,
        when the blind boys were too far gone.

Our last night, I knew it was going to be bad;
one of the customers had stopped me coming back
            from the men's room to ask why I didn't use hair tonic.
Then a big guy in suspenders and a plaid shirt
        and a cap that said "Sex is like snow,
you never know how many inches you're going to get"
            came up to the bandstand and asked,
"Y'all can play dat Potato Mash?"
    We knew our career was over anyway,

    so we began to laugh and make fun of him,
and he and his friends jumped up on stage
            to throw beer at us and turn over the drum kit.
The three of us who could see were frightened
        by these hairy bayou men with their great hard bellies
and their forearms big as Popeye's,
        but the blind boys didn't give a shit
and were ripped on bourbon and doughnuts anyway;
        howling, their fish-belly eyes red in the light

    from the beer signs, the blind boys lashed out
and began to hit the men and us and each other
            with the neck of the guitar and the drum sticks.
It was a fight in hell: "The Musicians versus the Fisherman,"
        like a myth from some country that had never developed
much of a culture. I got a cut lip and my first real hangover,
            and for days my parents heaped shame on my silent head.
But it was worth it to have seen the blind boys
        whip the ass of those tough fisherman;

for sure, they did the Potato Mash. Later we got more bourbon
and more doughnuts and had a real party. We sang and threw up,
          and one of the blind boys cried for his mother.
That was our only good moment—our last. On the ride home,
      we were a lyrical and pantheistic group of fellows,
and our music was *plus vague et plus soluble dans l'air*,
        according to the formula of the poet Verlaine,
son-in-law of Madame Mauté de Fleurville,
      Debussy's first teacher and herself a student of Chopin.